HOW MANY SUBJECTS?

HOW MANY SUBJECTS?

Statistical Power Analysis in Research

HELENA CHMURA KRAEMER
and SUE THIEMANN

Foreword by Victor H. Denenberg

SAGE PUBLICATIONS
The International Professional Publishers
Newbury Park   London   New Delhi

For information address:

SAGE Publications, Inc.
2455 Teller Road
Newbury Park, California 91320

SAGE Publications Ltd.
6 Bonhill Street
London EC2A 4PU
United Kingdom

SAGE Publications India Pvt. Ltd.
M-32 Market
Greater Kailash I
New Delhi 110 048 India

Printed in the United States of America

Library of Congress Cataloging-in-Publication Data

Kraemer, Helena Chmura.
   How many subjects?

   Bibliography: p.
   1. Research—Statistical methods. I. Thiemann,
Sue. II. Title. III. Title: Statistical power
analysis in research.
Q180.55.S7K73 1987   001.4'22   87-16575
ISBN 0-8039-2949-8

   93 94 10 9

CONTENTS

Foreword

This book fills a large gap in the applied statistics literature and, at the same time, provides empirical researchers with the means to quickly determine a valuable piece of information, namely: what sample size is needed for a particular study.

It is often not fully appreciated that in a statistical analysis there are *two* hypotheses under consideration. The *null hypothesis* assumes that the variable being investigated is without effect, and the data are given the opportunity to disprove the assumption. If one can reject the null hypothesis, then the *alternative hypothesis*—which is the reason that the investigator did the study—is accepted. The focus in applied statistics has been primarily upon assessing the null hypothesis, while consideration of the alternative hypothesis (i.e., the research hypothesis) has been neglected. Thus we can readily answer the question:

If the null hypothesis is true, how often are we likely to reject it?

We know that the error in rejecting the null hypothesis when true is called the *alpha* error and is given by the level of significance chosen by the investigator (usually the .05 or .01 levels, although other values may be used). However, we generally cannot answer the question:

If the alternative hypothesis is true, how often are we likely to reject it?

The error in rejecting the alternative hypothesis when true is called the *beta* error. We want that value to be as small as possible. The value 1 – *beta* is called the *power* of the test of significance and we wish that value to be as large as possible. The purpose of this book is to show the researcher how to set power for any study *prior to the initiation of the investigation*.

The lack of emphasis upon power in statistical texts is

unfortunate since the researcher's interest and efforts are aimed at establishing the validity of the alternative hypothesis. The investigator's concern may be expressed as follows:

> On the assumption that my research hypothesis is correct, what do I need to do to demonstrate that fact?

In part, the action one takes is a function of one's approach to the research question. Experimentalists control as many variables as possible, work with homogeneous subject pools (whether animal or human), carefully manipulate their independent variable(s), try to test their subjects within a relatively narrow time frame, etc. Those doing correlational studies carefully define their population and their methods of sampling, seek a wide range of individual differences, establish reliability of their measuring instruments, pretest their procedures, etc.

Researchers are very good at dealing with methodological and procedural issues in their investigation. However, they quite frequently fail to address a major statistical issue that is of direct concern to them: On the assumption that the research hypothesis is true, it is necessary that the investigator *determine the sample size (N) needed to give this hypothesis a reasonable chance of being proven correct.*

A power analysis of one's planned investigation provides the researcher with the N needed, and this is the major topic addressed by Kraemer and Thiemann in this text. To determine N, several questions must be answered. The first is:

> On the assumption that my research hypothesis is true, for the parameter of interest to me (usually a mean, a percentage, or a correlation coefficient), by how much do I expect my major research group to differ from some control group or reference value?

An alternative way of phrasing this is:

On the assumption that my research hypothesis is true, for the parameter of interest to me, what is the minimal value by which my research group must differ from some control group or reference value for me to be satisfied that I have established the validity of my hypothesis?

In order to answer this question in either form, the investigator needs to have conducted a preliminary study from which quantitative data are obtained estimating the parameter of interest (e.g., mean, percentage, correlation coefficient) and also estimating the variability of that statistic. The expected quantitative difference (e.g., a difference between a control mean and an experimental mean) is then divided by the measure of variability (e.g., the standard deviation), and the resulting value is called a *critical effect size* by Kraemer and Thiemann. Having obtained the critical effect size the next question that the researcher must answer is:

On the assumption that my research hypothesis is true, what probability would I like to assign to this investigation for obtaining a significant result (i.e., rejecting the null hypothesis)?

The answer to this question specifies the *power* of the test of significance. One's initial response is to choose a power value around .99 to be virtually certain of demonstrating significance if the alternative hypothesis is true. However, that is usually impossible because the number of subjects required per group to satisfy the requirement that power be .99 is almost certainly going to be prohibitive. Thus one settles for a lesser value, generally in the .7-.9 range.

The final piece of information needed is the decision rule concerning rejection of the null hypothesis. Is *alpha* set at .05 or .01? Is this a one-tailed or a two-tailed test?

With this information the researcher can enter the tables given by Kraemer and Theimann and determine the N needed to satisfy the power specifications of the experiment.

If this book only presented the reader with a straight-forward set of procedures for determining N for any particular research design, it would have fulfilled its mission successfully. But the book does more. In the course of discussing different designs, the authors make note of important points that are of value to the empirical researcher. These include: the conditions under which a repeated measures design will be more or less efficient than a cross-sectional design; the considerations involved in deciding whether to match or stratify subjects; the selection of variables for a multiple regression analysis; the value of equal (or near equal) N in analysis of variance designs; how to insure, in a correlational study, that the study will be valid; and the N required to make a reasonably rigorous test of one hypothesis using the chi-square technique.

This book has much to offer the careful and interested reader.

—Victor H. Denenberg,
University of Connecticut
Storrs, CT

Acknowledgment

We wish to thank the many researchers at Stanford University who have made us aware of the importance of cost-effective research, especially those in the Department of Psychiatry and Behavioral Sciences. We are grateful to the NIMH for the generous grant (MH-30854) which made the work possible. The kind encouragement of Jacob Cohen, whose earlier work on power calculations remains invaluable, is also gratefully acknowledged. Finally, we wish to thank Pamela Elliott for her patience, good humor, and tireless assistance in preparing the manuscript.

CHAPTER

1

Introduction

"How large a sample size must I have?" "Which approach should I take in designing my experiment?" "Which measure should I use, and which test to analyze my data?" "Will I have enough power with only the 20 (or 50 or 100) subjects available to me?"

Statistical consultants are frequently asked questions such as these by researchers in all fields—education, psychology, sociology, medicine, etc.—and such questions are often difficult to answer. Both the frequency and the difficulty of these questions are related to a single fact: In their training, researchers tend to be given a very cursory exposure to the concept of statistical power, and even more limited instruction in the applications of this concept. As a result, they are generally unable to answer such questions themselves. What is more, they can rarely anticipate the insights and the information a statistician needs to answer the questions completely and accurately.

Part of the problem of teaching power to researchers lies in the mathematical complexity of the topic. Although, in principle, deriving power is as straightforward as deriving a significance level, researchers are routinely trained to deal with significance level, but rarely with power. Within the time constraints of an applied statistics course, it is difficult enough to introduce the normal, central-t, χ^2, and F-distributions essential to standard statistical tests, much less the noncentral distributions necessary to power calculations. Consequently, the noncentral distributions are simply omitted from the curriculum.

The one exception to date has been the suggested strategy of using Cohen's (1977) book on power analysis as a supplementary text in an intermediate course in applied statistics. Well written though it is, Cohen's book is both long and difficult even for highly motivated researchers. Since his tables are structured so differently one from another, how tests interrelate is not apparent. Consequently, it is difficult to use in comparing different design strategies or different test choices.

But mathematical complexity is not the only problem. Power considerations are an integral part of planning a research project, a process that involves not only formal training, but also considerable experience in a particular research field. Planning a study involves:

—Specification of research goals in precise and realistic terms.

—Identification of the design and measurement options available to address the research questions.

—Evaluation of the resources (time, personnel and funding) available to the project.

Statistical power considerations are only then used to compare the potential consequences of such alternatives and to guide the selection of the most feasible and cost-effective choice in a particular research setting.

Specifying realistic goals, identifying design options, and evaluating resources are skills not easily conveyed in coursework, particularly not in a course on statistical methods, and particularly not early in research training, when such a course is usually presented.

What can be done, however, is to introduce a single method appropriate for calculating power for a wide variety of different tests. This method has already been presented in the context of teaching statistics (Kraemer, 1985) but is presented here in extended form for use by nonstatisticians. For the tests commonly used by researchers, we provide detailed instructions for calculating the effect size required by power calculations and for using one table to estimate sample size or power in the various test situations. This innovation eliminates most of the mathematical complexity of power calculations, allowing researchers to focus on the broader design and measurement issues involved in statistical power.

These design and measurement decisions ultimately determine the cost of a study. Thus a thorough understanding of statistical power not only allows researchers to compute sample sizes, it enables them to make the most efficient use of resources, an increasingly important consideration as funding in many fields grows more and more limited. The simplified sample size computations allow a clear comparison of the costs of various research strategies. We emphasize these cost considerations, as well as the feasibility of a number of alternative research designs.

In this presentation, Chapter 2 briefly reviews the general concepts of power and significance level, and Chapter 3 provides the theoretical justification for the use of a single table for a variety of tests. Beginning in Chapter 4, we will use the mock planning of a study to illustrate the ways in which power considerations are used to compare tests, designs, and measures. The mock planning will deal with a research project on the issue: Is coffee drinking dangerous to health? This is not a frivolous or trivial question. Coffee drinking has been implicated in hypertension (Whitsett et al., 1984), cardiovascular disease (Williams et al., 1985) and a number of cancers, including pancreatic (Binstock et al., 1983), ovarian (La Vecchia et al., 1984), bladder (Marrett et al., 1983), bowel (Phillips and Snowdon, 1983), and colon (Snowdon and Phillips, 1984). Yet most adults in the United States drink coffee on a daily basis, and many drink three or more cups per day. If, in fact, coffee is dangerous, there are widespread social and economic, as well as medical, implications. Should warning labels be required, or should coffee be removed from the markets? Should there be strict limits on advertising? Should campaigns to reduce coffee-drinking be instituted? Similar problems in recent years with cyclamates, saccharin, and cigarettes demonstrate that such issues involve not just medical researchers but social scientists in all fields, from economics to psychology.

We plan these mock studies just as a researcher might, beginning with preliminary evidence and ending with a firm sample size recommendation. The proposals, however, are selected to be the simplest, lacking the sophistication a medical researcher, a sociologist, a psychologist or an economist would bring to this problem. Such an approach provides realistic and concrete examples of sample size calculations and highlights the design and measurement issues researchers must consider each and every time they plan a study.

CHAPTER
2

General Concepts

2.1 Introduction

The scientific method requires that the researchers proposing a theory (e.g., drinking coffee is dangerous to health) put that theory to empirical tests. *Statistical hypothesis testing* is one such formalized empirical test, in structure analogous to the Anglo-Saxon system of trial by jury. In this trial, the researchers play the role of the prosecution, the collection of data plays the role of the trial procedure itself, and the statistical test plays the role of the jury in deciding the verdict.

The basic overall principle is that the researchers' theory is considered false until demonstrated beyond reasonable doubt to be true, just as the accused is presumed innocent in law: Until the evidence demonstrates the danger of drinking coffee, we assume that drinking coffee is safe. This is expressed as an assumption that the *null hypothesis*, the contradiction of the researchers' theory, is true. Thus the null hypothesis in our mock trial is that drinking coffee is safe. What is considered a "reasonable" doubt is called the *significance level*. By convention in scientific research, a "reasonable" level of remaining doubt is one below either 5% or 1%.

The researchers, in the role of the prosecution, evaluate the preliminary evidence (literature review, case histories, theoretical considerations, pilot studies, etc.) and decide whether or not the case is important enough, and whether or not preliminary evidence convincing enough, to bring the hypothesis to trial, i.e., to test the hypothesis.

The researchers also formulate the trial strategy. They decide what design to use, which measure of response to use, the number and timing of measurements per subject, which test to use, and how many subjects to sample. All of these decisions affect how likely the evidence is to be "convincing beyond reasonable doubt"—the *power* of the trial.

For example, in our mock trial, we must somehow measure coffee-drinking. We could do this by asking a retrospective self-report of each subject (e.g., "Normally, how many cups of coffee do you drink per day?"). Alternatively, we could ask each subject to keep a diary of coffee-drinking for a week or two, or we could directly monitor or measure caffeine intake in some way. Similarly, we could assess the health of the subjects by requiring a complete physical exam including X-rays and lab tests. We could do this once, or every six months for 10 years. Or we could have a medical professional take a health history and inventory, and do this once or periodically. Or we could use some self-report system such as the Cornell Medical Index (Brodman et al., 1949), and do this once or periodically.

Clearly, using self-reports of coffee-drinking and health only once (cross-sectional study) will be cheaper than using professional assessment or doing a longitudinal study. Which decisions we make, and whether we apply these decisions to 50 or 100 or 500 subjects, will obviously affect how convincing the result will be, and how costly and time-consuming the study.

A *statistical test* defines a rule that, when applied to the data, determines whether the null hypothesis can be rejected, i.e., whether the evidence is convincing beyond reasonable doubt. Both the significance level and the power of the test are derived by calculating with what probability a positive verdict would be obtained (the null hypothesis rejected) if the same trial were run over and over again. To obtain the significance level, these hypothetical reruns are done when the null hypothesis is taken to be true. To obtain power, these hypothetical reruns are done when the researchers' theory is true. The student in an introductory course is, in most cases, given the rule (the statistical test) and is told the circumstances in which the rule applies (the assumptions) but is not taught how to derive each test (how the reruns are actually done).

For a test to be a *valid* 5% or 1% test, the computation of significance level must be correct. Such computations involve certain assumptions about the nature of the population. If a certain test were used when the population does not meet these assumptions, the test may be *invalid*: a mistrial. Frequently, however, the test is derived under a number of specific assumptions, but only a few are crucial to the validity of the test. Tests having few assumptions crucial to their validity are known as *robust* tests.

For the computation of power, the researchers must have developed from the preliminary evidence a *critical effect size*, a measure of how strong the theory must minimally be to be "important to society." So, for example, the very minimal increase a subject may have on the Cornell Medical Index is one point (on a 195-point scale). Previous evidence indicates that for every 10 years, the index increases about three to four points. The difference between a healthy subject and one with an acute illness is about five to six points. With this as background information, how small an increase in the index would occasion social concerns about the safety of coffee-drinking? Certainly no less than one point, but perhaps as much as 10 points would be required to motivate social and economic strictures on coffee-drinking. Such background information is used to estimate a *critical effect size*. The specification of the critical effect size is based on the researchers' understanding and knowledge of their field, supplemented by the preliminary evidence available, and reflects both population characteristics and the proposed research design. It is important to realize that one cannot plan a cost-effective study without any background or preliminary information—any more than a prosecutor would institute a trial by jury without evidence to back the charge.

Changing designs, changing the measure to be used, or choosing one valid test rather than another changes the definition of the "effect size." Furthermore, the critical effect size is population-specific as well as measurement-specific. What the critical effect size is for 20-year-old men might be very different from that for 50-year-old women. What the critical effect size will be using the CMI might be very different from using another health index or a score generated from a physician's report. The researchers may well consider different designs and measures before launching the trial. They then choose the strategy which seems most powerful, or one which has sufficient power but is least costly.

Researchers should remember several points. There is a difference between preliminary evidence and the trial itself. One cannot formulate a theory by examining some evidence, and then test it on the same material (post hoc testing). Preliminary evidence is meant to convince the researchers that a trial is worthwhile, but the trial must be run on a hypothesis that is stated a priori.

Also, the question of power enters consideration only in planning a study, not after the study is done, and the verdict is in. If the verdict is negative, i.e., a nonsignificant or nonconvincing result, then the researchers' theory was inadequate, or their evaluation of preliminary evidence was faulty, or their design, measurement, analysis, or sample size decisions were faulty. In short, somewhere along the line, decisions were inadequate. One might well use the evidence of this trial as preliminary evidence in planning a better future trial, but no "post hoc" power calculations change the outcome of this trial. There is some flavor of double jeopardy in a researchers' report that although result of trial is negative (a nonsignificant result), the "trend" was in the right direction and supported the researchers' theory.

On the other hand, if the verdict is positive, the decisions were willy-nilly good enough. (Moses's Principle of the Blunt Ax: "If the ax chopped down the tree, it was sharp enough." Quoted in Goldstein, 1964, p. 62.)

2.2 Introduction to the Power Table

In the Master Table (see pages 105-112) are four sections corresponding to one- and two-tailed 5% and 1% tests of significance. The 5% and 1% are the most commonly used levels of significance. Whether the test is one- or two-tailed is determined by how the researchers' theory is formulated. In our mock trial, the theory states that drinking coffee is harmful—a one-tailed theory. If we had instead theorized that drinking coffee changes the health status for better or for worse, the theory would have been two-tailed.

The columns of each section of the table relate to various levels of power (10% to 99%), or probability of obtaining a significant result (i.e., rejecting the null hypothesis), for the statistical test. In the trial analogy, power is the likelihood of a guilty verdict. The rows relate to the critical effect size, Δ, that is in each case determined from the researcher's knowledge of the field and from preliminary evidence. The index Δ has values ranging from 0 to 1. A value of 0 (or less) means that the researchers' theory is false. A value of 1.00 is an "open and shut case." The critical effect size lies somewhere between these extremes and reflects design and population parameters, but not the sample size.

In the body of the table are listed numbers designated ν. These numbers correspond to sample size in ways determined by the design of the study, but do not involve any population parameters.

A "population parameter" is some numerical characteristic of the population (mean, variance, etc.), which is unknown and is to be estimated using a sample from the population. A "design parameter" reflects the choice of the researcher, for example, as to how to allocate subjects to groups (equal numbers), or how many observations per subject to take $(1, 2, \ldots)$ and the spacing or circumstances of these observations (every 6 months, every year, after 10 years). The sample size is, of course, the total number of subjects sampled from the population.

For each test, instructions will be provided to compute Δ and ν in terms of the design and population parameters. Once these are defined for a test, one can use the appropriate section of the Master Table by specifying any two of the three entries (i.e., power, critical effect size, and sample size) and reading off the third.

For practice at this stage, regard ν as the sample size and follow these examples. Then, for example, to have 90% power for a 5% one-tailed test with a critical effect size of 0.4, one would need 49 subjects. If the test were to be a two-tailed 5% test, one would need 60 subjects. For one- and two-tailed 1% tests, the numbers would be 74 and 84. If the effect were smaller, say 0.10, these numbers would be 852, 1045, 1295, 1480. If one were satisfied to have 80% chance of success, the number would be 36 for a one-tailed 5% test with a critical effect size of 0.4, and 616 with a critical effect size of 0.1.

From such exercises, we learn the following "facts of life":

—The more stringent the significance level, the greater the necessary sample size. More subjects are needed for a 1% level test than for a 5% level test.

—Two-tailed tests require larger sample sizes than one-tailed tests. Assessing two directions at the same time requires a greater investment.

—The smaller the critical effect size, the larger the necessary sample size. Subtle effects require greater efforts.

—The larger the power required, the larger the necessary sample size. Greater protection from failure requires greater effort.

—The smaller the sample size, the smaller the power, i.e., the greater the chance of failure (a hung jury or a not-guilty verdict).

—If one proposed to go to trial with a sample size of 20 or fewer subjects, one must be willing to take a high risk of failure, or be operating in an area in which the critical effect size is large indeed.

—To achieve 99% power for a critical effect size of 0.01 (as most students initially specify), a researcher must be prepared to recruit and process more than 150,000 subjects. The acid test of whether an effect size of 0.01 is, in fact, "important to society" is whether society is prepared to fund a study requiring 150,000 subjects. Specification of the critical effect size and the required power, we repeat, must be realistic, not idealistic.

In the Master Table, no values of ν are listed that are less than 10. The minimum sample size necessary for the credibility of a study differs from field to field. Seldom is an opinion survey done with fewer than 1,000 subjects. Sociological studies and epidemiological studies rarely use fewer than several hundred subjects. Clinical trials in medicine with 10-20 subjects per groups are frequently seen, and in some areas of behavioral research published peer-reviewed studies can be based on a sample size of one. To some extent, the differences in the minimum acceptable sample size reflect the types of questions, designs, measures and analyses that are used in a particular field, and therefore the sample sizes necessary for reasonable power. To some extent, it is simply custom. The decision to list no sample sizes less than 10 in Table 1, however, is due not so much to what researchers consider an adequate sample size for publication but to a concern about the accuracy of power calculations when sample sizes are too small.

2.3 Statistical Considerations

An important question is whether it is, in fact, possible to compile a single table appropriate for a wide selection of common statistical tests. In Chapter 3 is an explanation and derivation (for the one-tailed tests) of the Master Table. This derivation may not be of interest to nonstatistical researchers and is designed so that it might be skipped without compromising the understanding of what follows.

However, a few key points should be noted. The values of ν in the Master Table should be regarded as approximate. In fact, for certain tests (intraclass correlation, homogeneity of variance with balanced independent samples), the results are exact under the assumptions on which the tests are based. For others (correlation coefficients, t-tests) they are likely to be very accurate, for they are based on approximation procedures known to be very accurate (Kraemer, 1973; Boomsma, 1977; Chaubey and Mudholkar, 1978). However, in general, it is better policy to always regard them as approximations. First, in many cases they *are* approximations and not the best of all available ones. Second, in practice we will use linear or even "eye-ball" interpolation in the tables. This compromises accuracy even for the exact results. Third, and perhaps most important, it is seldom known with certainty that the assumptions underlying the test are precisely met. Finally, as we have seen, the critical effect size is itself only an estimate. At best, the results can only be as accurate as the estimates and assumptions are true.

In Chapters 4 through 9, we demonstrate power calculations for a variety of different statistical tests. In every case, we first describe the critical effect size for the test (Δ), that minimum effect considered important to detect, using information from previous work to estimate its magnitude. For instance, earlier or pilot studies may provide estimates of means and standard deviations in the populations of interest. We also demonstrate how the ν from the Master Table relates to the sample size our test requires. The Summary Table provides a convenient summary of these results for a number of common tests.

The Pivotal Case: Intraclass Correlation

3.1 An Intraclass Correlation Test

Suppose (X_i, Y_i), $i = 1, 2, \ldots, n$, are drawn from a bivariate normal population with correlation coefficient ρ and equal variances. The maximum likelihood estimate of ρ is the intraclass correlation coefficient (r_I) (Kraemer, 1975). Whatever the value of ρ:

$$u = u(r_I, \rho) = (r_I - \rho)/(1 - r_I \rho) \qquad (3.1.1)$$

has a distribution that depends only on $\nu = n - 1$, specifically:

$$\nu^{1/2} u/(1 - u^2)^{1/2} \sim t_\nu, \qquad (3.1.2)$$

the t-distribution with ν degrees of freedom. The percentile points of the u-distribution (3.1.2) are easily computed from the percentile points of the t-distribution:

$$u_{\nu\alpha} = t_{\nu\alpha}/(t_{\nu\alpha}^2 + \nu)^{1/2}. \qquad (3.1.3)$$

These values are tabled and readily available (e.g., Pearson and Hartley, 1962, Table 13, p. 138).

To test the null hypothesis H_0: $\rho \le 0$ vs. A: $\rho > 0$ one would reject H_0 at the α level if:

$$u(r_I, 0) = r_I \ge u_{\nu\alpha}. \qquad (3.1.4)$$

The power of this test (P) at any critical effect size $\rho > 0$ is the solution to the equation (Kraemer, 1975):

$$\Delta = (u_{\nu\alpha} - u_{\nu P})/(1 - u_{\nu\alpha} u_{\nu P}), \qquad (3.1.5)$$

where

$$\Delta = \rho.$$

The Master Table presents the exact solution to (3.1.5) (ν rounded to the next higher integer value) and therefore to any problem concerning power, the solution to which depends on a distribution such as that specified in (3.1.1) and (3.1.2).

3.2 The ANOVA Approach to the Intraclass Correlation Test

Let us now look at this same problem somewhat differently. It is known that the computation of this intraclass correlation coefficient may be based on the Two-Way (Subjects $\times$ 2 Tests) Analysis of Variance (ANOVA) (e.g., Haggard, 1958; Bartko, 1976). The F-test for subjects in this analysis, $\hat{F}$, can be shown to be:

$$\hat{F} = (1 + r_I)/(1 - r_I). \tag{3.2.1}$$

From ANOVA theory (subjects a random effect):

$$\hat{F} \sim \lambda F_{\nu,\nu}, \quad \lambda = (1 + \rho)/(1 - \rho). \tag{3.2.2}$$

Testing H_0: $\rho \leq 0$ vs. A: $\rho > 0$ is absolutely equivalent to testing H_0: $\lambda \leq 1$ vs. A: $\lambda > 1$. The test based on $\hat{F}$ is exactly equivalent to that based on r_I.

What this means is that for any test of H_0: $\lambda \leq 1$ vs. A: $\lambda > 1$, based on a statistic $\hat{F}$ having the distribution described in (3.2.2), one can compute $\nu = n - 1$ and $\Delta = (\lambda - 1)/(\lambda + 1)$, and use the Master Table to execute exact power calculations.

3.3 Normal Approximation to the Intraclass Theory

Let us look at this problem in yet a third way. From (3.2.2),

$$0.5 \ln \left[(1 + r_1)/(1 - r_1) \right] \sim 0.5 \ln \left[(1 + \rho)/(1 - \rho) \right]$$

$$+ 0.5 \ln F_{\nu,\nu}. \qquad (3.3.1)$$

The transformation $Z(r) = 0.5 \ln[(1 + r)/(1 - r)]$ is well-known as Fisher's transformation of the correlation coefficient (Fisher, 1921). The random variable $0.5 \ln F_{\nu,\nu}$ has approximately a normal distribution with mean 0 and variance $1/(h-1)$ where h is the harmonic mean of the two degrees of freedom (Cochran, 1940). Here $h = n - 1$.

   Again, what this means is that for any test of H_0: $Z(\Delta) \leq 0$ vs. A: $Z(\Delta) > 0$ based on a statistic Z such that:

$$Z \sim N(Z(\Delta), 1/N) \qquad (3.3.2)$$

where N depends in some way on n, one can compute $\nu = N + 1$ and Δ and use the Master Table to execute approximate power calculations.

   The case of the intraclass correlation coefficient is pivotal, for it furnishes a link between test of correlation coefficients, of variance ratios, and of mean differences. These are the three general problems that underlie most of the common test procedures introduced in an elementary statistical course.

3.4 Non-Central t

   Now suppose one had a situation in which one wished to test the hypothesis H_0: $\delta \leq 0$ vs. A: $\delta > 0$ using a test statistic T such that:

$$T \sim t'_\nu(\sqrt{N}\delta) \qquad (3.4.1)$$

where t' is the non-central t-distribution with ν degrees of freedom and non-centrality parameter $\sqrt{N}\delta$. It is known that

$$T/(T^2 + \nu)^{1/2} \tag{3.4.2}$$

is approximately distributed as is the intraclass correlation coefficient (Kraemer and Paik, 1979) with

$$\rho = N^{1/2}\delta/(N\delta^2 + \nu)^{1/2} = \delta/(\delta^2 + \nu/N)^{1/2} \approx \delta/(\delta^2 + d)^{1/2}. \tag{3.4.3}$$

If δ and $d = \nu/N$ depended only on population and design parameters, then one could use the Master Table with:

$$\Delta = \delta/(\delta^2 + d)^{1/2}. \tag{3.4.4}$$

3.5 Variance Ratios

Suppose one had a situation in which one wished to test the hypothesis $H_0: \lambda \leq 1$ vs. $A: \lambda > 1$ using a test statistic $\hat{F}$ such that:

$$\hat{F} \sim \lambda F_{\nu_1, \nu_2} \tag{3.5.1}$$

where ν_1, ν_2 depend only on sample size and design, and λ on population characteristics and on design. If ν_1 and ν_2 were not too disparate or provided both were large, this distribution could be approximated by

$$\hat{F} \sim \lambda F_{h,h} \tag{3.5.2}$$

where h is the harmonic mean of ν_1 and ν_2 (Cochran, 1940). Now one could use the Master Table with

$$\nu = h, \quad \Delta = (\lambda - 1)/(\lambda + 1). \tag{3.5.3}$$

CHAPTER
4

Equality of Means:
z- and t-Tests,
Balanced ANOVA

The sample mean is probably the most familiar of all
statistical estimates, and tests of the mean are usually the first
ones taught in an elementary statistics course. These tests
cover a wide variety of situations, corresponding to the many
ways in which a researcher might choose to investigate the level
of a variable in one or more populations.

4.1 Single-Sample Test,
Variance Known: z-test

If the responses were normally distributed with mean
μ and *known* variance σ^2, we reject H_0: $\mu = \mu_0$ if the quantity
$(\overline{X} - \mu_0)/\sigma$, where $\overline{X}$ is the observed sample mean and μ_0 a
specified value (often zero), is greater than the α-level critical
value of the standard normal distribution ($Z\alpha$). This is the
familiar z-test, usually the first test discussed in an elementary
statistics course. Here, for use in the Master Table:

$$\delta = (\mu - \mu_0)/\sigma, \tag{4.1}$$

$$Z(\Delta) = \delta, \text{ i.e.,}$$

$$\Delta = (e^{2\delta} - 1)/(e^{2\delta} + 1)$$

$$n = \nu - 1.$$

For example, from previous examination of the Cornell Medical Index (Gordon et al., 1959), it appears that
healthy men in their forties have a CMI with mean about 8 and
standard deviation about 7 ($\mu_0 = 8$, $\sigma = 7$) and the CMI tends to
increase 3-4 points (say 3.5 points) for each 10 years of age.
With that background, if coffee were indeed dangerous
to health, a sample of men in their forties who are heavy coffee
drinkers (say three or more cups per day on self-report) would
be expected to have a mean CMI well above 8 ($\mu_0 = 8$). If we
sampled n such men and assumed that the standard deviation

is what it appears to be in the general population ($\sigma = 7$), we could use a single-sample z-test to test this theory.

What would be an important enough difference to warrant concern? A one-point difference (on the 195-point CMI scale) would be minimal and probably not enough to warrant taking any public health action to reduce coffee-drinking. But a 3.5-point difference corresponds to "aging" subjects in terms of their CMI about 10 years and might occasion public concern. In this case, $\mu - \mu_0 = 3.5$ and with $\sigma = 7$: $\delta = 0.5$. Then from (4.1) $\Delta = 0.46$. For a one-tailed test at the 5% level with 90% power, the Master Table shows that $\nu = 36$ (interpolating between 38 and 30). Since $n = \nu - 1$, the necessary sample size would be 35. For a 5% one-tailed test with 99% power, $\nu = 66$ (between 69 and 54), and thus the sample size would be 65.

This is the one case when doing exact power calculations is as easy as using the tabled values. For an α-level test, with power P, the exact sample size necessary to detect a value of δ is

$$n = (z_\alpha - Z_p)^2 / \delta^2.$$

In Table 4.1 appear the exact values of n and the values obtained by linear interpolation in the Master Table. There are minor differences in the recommended sample size. Once again, be reminded that power calculations yield approximations, not exact values, both because of the nature of the calculation and the estimates of effect sizes involved in the calculation.

4.2. Single-Sample or Matched Pair t-test

If the responses are normally distributed with mean μ and unknown variance σ^2, we reject H_0: $\mu \leq \mu_0$ if:

$$(\overline{X} - \mu_0)/s \geq t_{n-1,\alpha}$$

TABLE 4.1
Exact and Approximate Calculations for the z-test:
Sample Sizes for 90 and 99% Power, 5% one-tailed

		90% power		99% power	
δ	Δ	exact	approximate	exact	approximate
0.1	0.10	857	851	1578	1567
0.2	0.20	215	209	395	384
0.3	0.29	96	97	176	178
0.4	0.38	54	54	99	99
0.5	0.46	35	36	64	65
0.6	0.54	24	25	44	45
0.7	0.60	18	18	33	33
0.8	0.66	14	15	25	26
0.9	0.72	11	11	20	20
1.0	0.76	9	<10	16	17

where $\overline{X}$ is the sample mean and s^2, the sample variance. Here:

$$\delta = (\mu - \mu_0)/\sigma, \tag{4.2}$$

$$\Delta = \delta/(\delta^2 + 1)^{1/2},$$

$$n = \nu + 1.$$

In the z-test example above, we used the background information to estimate the standard deviation in the population ($\sigma = 7$) for use in the test, as well as to calculate the critical effect size. Background studies, however, are done at a different time and a different place, and this information may not apply to the sample now under study. If this standard deviation were in error, the test we propose to apply (the z-test) might not be valid. Consequently, although we must use the background information to estimate the critical effect size in planning our study, we might hesitate to stake the validity of our final test result on this value. Instead, we would use a single-sample t-test, in which we *estimate* the standard deviation in the sample we obtain, rather than using a value from a potentially different population.

In this case, δ remains 0.5. However Δ is now different (4.2), because this is a different test. The value now is 0.45, not 0.46 as above, when the variance was known. This means, of course, that the necessary sample size will increase somewhat. From the Master Table, for a 5% one-tailed test with 90% power, the value of ν now is 38, and since now n = ν + 1, the necessary sample size is 39, not 35 as above. To protect the validity of the test, we are obliged to obtain 4 more subjects— not a bad price to insure validity.

Table 4.2 shows the approximate sample size for the z-test, and that for the t-test, for 5% level tests with 90% and 99% power for a range of σ values. Clearly, the necessary sample size is always somewhat greater for the t-test than for the z-test, but the small increase is well worthwhile to protect the validity of the test.

4.3. Two-Sample t-test

The two-sample t-test is probably the most commonly used statistical test. Suppose a proportion p of a total of n subjects come from one group and a proportion q from a second group (p + q = 1). The scores in both groups are taken to be normally distributed with the same variance, but the first group has mean μ_x and the second group mean μ_y. Here $H_0: \mu_x \geq \mu_y$. The two-sample t-test rejects H_0 when:

$$n(pq)^{1/2}(\overline{X} - \overline{Y})/s \geq t_{n-2,\alpha},$$

where $\overline{X}$ and $\overline{Y}$ are the two sample means and s^2 is the pooled within-group variance. One can then use the Master Table with:

$$\delta = (\mu_x - \mu_y)/\sigma, \qquad (4.3)$$

$$\Delta = \delta/(\delta^2 + 1/pq)^{1/2},$$

$$n = \nu + 2.$$

The parameter δ has been called "Glass's effect size" and has enjoyed extensive use in meta-analyses in recent years (Hedges and Olkin, 1985). In that context, researchers have been urged to publish either the values of Glass's effect size for their own research projects, or to publish the descriptive statistics (i.e., the means and standard deviations) necessary to the calculations of Glass's effect size. Routine publication of such information would facilitate not only meta-analyses but also cost-effective planning of future research in related areas.

From the formula for Δ in (4.3), we see that balance (the values of p and q) affects the power of the two-sample t-test. If the group sizes are equal (a balanced design: p = q = 1/2), then the critical effect size is maximal. As seen in Table 4.3, the greater the imbalance (as either p or q nears zero), the smaller the critical effect size. To achieve maximal power from a fixed sample size, equalize the group sizes. Alternatively, if the group sizes are unbalanced, the necessary total sample size must be larger.

For a δ of 0.5, for example, moving from perfect balance (p = q = 0.5) to a 90-10 split (i.e., 90% in one group, 10% in the other), the critical effect size decreases from 0.24 to 0.15. Thus, for a 5% one-tailed test and 80% power, a 50-50 split requires 107 subjects, a 70-30 split requires 127 subjects (125 + 2), an 80-20 split requires 154 subjects (152 + 2), and a 90-10 split, 274 subjects (272 + 2).

From this result and the effect sizes listed in Table 4.3, it is clear that power is maximized with an even, 50-50, split, but the increase in sample size necessary with slight imbalance (60-40 or 70-30) is not daunting. With an extreme split (80-20 or 90-10 or worse), however, the critical effect size rapidly

TABLE 4.2
σ^2 known vs σ^2 unknown: Sample sizes for single-sample
z- and t-tests for 90 and 99% power, 5% one-tailed

	Δ σ^2 known	Δ σ^2 unknown	90% power		99% power	
δ			N σ^2 known	N σ^2 unknown	N σ^2 known	N σ^2 unknown
0.1	0.10	0.10	851	853	1567	1569
0.2	0.20	0.20	209	211	384	386
0.3	0.29	0.29	97	99	178	180
0.4	0.38	0.37	54	60	99	108
0.5	0.46	0.45	36	39	65	70
0.6	0.54	0.51	25	30	45	53
0.7	0.60	0.57	18	23	33	41
0.8	0.66	0.62	15	19	26	33
0.9	0.72	0.67	11	16	20	27
1.0	0.76	0.71	<10	14	17	23

approaches zero, and the sample sizes become very large indeed.

This is one reason that epidemiological studies usually require very large sample sizes, frequently in the thousands. Such studies often compare groups with and without a certain disorder or disease that is relatively rare in the general population. The result is a gross imbalance in group sizes, which necessitates a very large sample size for enough power to detect even quite large effects. In other contexts such as medical clinical trials or psychological experiments, sample sizes need be nowhere near as large, for these sample sizes tend to be more balanced.

In the earlier examples, using the z-test or the single-sample t-test, we compared coffee drinkers with a "historical control group." However, such a control group, designed from a study done in another time and locale, may not well represent what is true in the time or locale of the current research. Over the years since that study was done, 40-year-old men may have grown healthier (or less so), or more variable (or less so). If any of these changes have occurred, using either the single-sample z-test, or the single-sample t-test may be invalid in the current study. Again, the background information must suffice to help plan the study, but risking an invalid test result by depending on this information for the final study result may not be a sound strategy.

Instead, we can obtain a concurrent control group of non-coffee drinkers against which to compare a group of coffee drinkers. As above, we will take as our critical value of Glass's effect $\delta = 0.5$.

If we proposed to sample a general population and simply discard those who are neither non-coffee drinkers nor heavy coffee drinkers by our definition, accepting the group sizes as they come, we are likely to end with an unbalanced sample. If, on the other hand, we recruit exactly the same number of coffee drinkers as non-coffee drinkers, we would

TABLE 4.3
Two-Sample t-test: Critical Effect Sizes (Δ) for Balanced (p = q = 0.5) and Unbalanced (p ≠ q) Group Sizes

	p, q =				
δ	*0.5*	*0.6* *0.4*	*0.7* *0.3*	*0.8* *0.2*	*0.9* *0.1*
0.1	0.05	0.05	0.05	0.04	0.03
0.2	0.10	0.10	0.09	0.08	0.06
0.3	0.15	0.15	0.14	0.12	0.09
0.4	0.20	0.19	0.18	0.16	0.12
0.5	0.24	0.24	0.22	0.20	0.15
0.6	0.29	0.28	0.27	0.23	0.18
0.7	0.33	0.32	0.31	0.27	0.21
0.8	0.37	0.36	0.34	0.30	0.23
0.9	0.41	0.40	0.38	0.34	0.26
1.0	0.45	0.44	0.42	0.37	0.29

end with a balanced sample. From the above, we see that in the unbalanced case, we might need 274 subjects as compared to 107 in the balanced case—not a trivial difference.

4.4 An Exercise in Planning

Often researchers must choose between various designs. For example, the following three designs could be used to answer the same question:

Option 1: The Single-Sample Pre-Post Design:

Healthy 20-year-old men who are non-coffee drinkers are recruited and their CMI measured at the baseline. They are then followed for 20 years. Only those subjects who take up coffee drinking in the interim period are retained for analysis.

For these subjects, the CMI is again measured at 40 years of age. A matched pair t-test is used to compare the change. (Keep in mind the cost of following those subjects for 20 years!)

Now on the basis of previous studies, the mean CMI in the general population should normally be about 6 points higher at the age of 40 than it was at the age of 20 ($\mu_2 - \mu_1 = 6$). We would use this information with:

$$\delta = (\mu_2 - \mu_1)/\sigma \, [2(1-\rho)]^{1/2}$$
$$\Delta = \delta/(\delta^2 + 1)^{1/2},$$
$$n = \nu + 1,$$

where μ_2 is the mean CMI for coffee drinkers at age 40, μ_1 is calculated here as the mean CMI at age 20 + 6, and ρ is the correlation coefficient between the CMI at 20 and that at 40.

Option 2: The Endpoint Study

Forty-year-old men, half of whom are coffee drinkers and half who are not, but none of whom drank coffee prior to the age of 20, are recruited into the study. Their CMIs are measured and a two-sample t-test is used to compare the two groups on this endpoint measure. (A much cheaper study than option 1: no 20-year follow-up.)

In this case

$$\delta = (\mu_2 - \mu_1)/\sigma,$$
$$\Delta = \delta/(\delta^2 + 4)^{1/2},$$
$$n = \nu + 2.$$

where μ_2 is the mean CMI of those who drink coffee and μ_1 is the mean CMI of those who do not.

Option 3: The Repeated Measures Design

Healthy 20-year-old men, none of whom are coffee drinkers, are recruited into the study. Their CMI is measured at baseline. They are then followed for 20 years, when an equal number of subjects who have taken up coffee drinking and who have remained abstainers are selected for study. Their CMI is again measured at 40 years of age. A two-sample t-test is used to compare the two groups on the pre-post change. (A very costly design, involving a 20-year follow-up and necessitating a sufficient number of recruits at baseline to yield the requisite sample size 20 years later.)

$$\delta = (\mu_2 - \mu_1)/\sigma \, [2(1-\rho)]^{1/2},$$

$$\Delta = \delta/(\delta^2 + 4)^{1/2},$$

$$n = \nu + 1.$$

where μ_2 is the mean change in CMI among those who drank coffee and μ_1 is the mean change in CMI among those who did not.

All responses are assumed to have equal within-group variance (σ^2), and the correlation between 20- and 40-year-old CMIs, ρ, is assumed to be the same in both the coffee-drinking and abstaining group.

Which design would you prefer if the decision were to be based strictly on statistical validity and power? Which would be most cost-effective?

Table 4.4 shows the critical effect sizes when the correlation (ρ) between the 20- and 40-year measures is 0.1, 0.5, and 0.9, and when Glass's effect size (δ) is 0.1, 0.5 and 1.0.

The pre-post study always has the maximal effect size, which means the minimum necessary sample size. However, this design may have questionable validity, for the value of μ_1 is based not on the present population but on a historical control group. If there were any question as to whether such an histori-

TABLE 4.4
Critical Effect Sizes (Δ) for Pre-Post, Endpoint,
and Repeated Measures Designs

δ	ρ	Pre-Post Δ	Endpoint Δ	Repeated Measures Δ
0.1	0.1	0.07	0.05	0.04
0.1	0.5	0.10	0.05	0.05
0.1	0.9	0.22	0.05	0.11
0.5	0.1	0.35	0.24	0.18
0.5	0.5	0.45	0.24	0.24
0.5	0.9	0.75	0.24	0.49
1.0	0.1	0.60	0.45	0.35
1.0	0.5	0.71	0.45	0.45
1.0	0.9	0.91	0.45	0.75

cal control group was appropriate, this would probably not be
the best choice, despite its apparently greater power.

When $\rho = 0.5$, the endpoint and repeated measures
designs have equal critical effect size and therefore require
equal sample size. However, these designs differ vastly in cost,
for the endpoint design requires only one measure per subject,
whereas the repeated measures requires two separated by 20
years of follow-up. Any additional measure takes up the time
of subjects and personnel and therefore increases cost, particularly, as in this case, when long follow-up is required to obtain
the repeated measures. In this case, the additional expenditure
for repeated measure design is wasted, for there is no resulting
increase in the effectiveness of the design.

When $\rho < 0.5$, the endpoint design has more power.
When $\rho > 0.5$ the repeated measures design does. In short,
when assessing a trait that is relatively stable over time and
characteristic of the subject, repeated measures will increase
power. When assessing a state (or an unstable trait), which

may characterize the subject at one point but does not persist over time, endpoint designs are preferable.

It is important for researchers to realize that there are no black-and-white answers to such design questions. Which is a better design always depends on the nature of the specific research question, as well as on the nature of the response in the population to be studied (humans). Such matters are better understood by the researcher who is expert in that field than by any consultant statistician, no matter how expert in the field of statistics. This is particularly true when the feasibility and cost of the three designs must be simultaneously considered—as they invariably must be.

4.5 Balanced Analysis of Variance (ANOVA)

The matched-pair t-test and the two-sample t-test are both designed to compare two means. There are many situations, however, when there are more than two means of simultaneous interest. In the Analysis of Variance (ANOVA) approach, factors, each measured at several levels, define a number of cells, the means of which are compared in the analysis.

In such cases, the researcher may consider the pairwise mean comparisons of specific interest, one at a time, and use either the two-sample or matched-pair t-test methods (as appropriate) to compute the necessary sample size required per cell. The maximal per cell sample size so computed is multiplied by the number of cells to give the necessary total sample size for a balanced ANOVA.

For example, a researcher may decide to simultaneously investigate the effects of drinking regular coffee, drinking only decaffeinated coffee, and not drinking coffee at all by sampling an equal number of subjects from each of these groups and measuring their CMIs. There are now three possible comparisons, or two-sample t-tests: regular coffee versus decaffeinated (R vs. D), regular coffee versus abstention (R vs. A), and decaffeinated coffee versus abstention (D vs. A). As before, we wish to detect a 3.5-point increase in the CMI scores of regular coffee drinkers over abstainers, and this is also the effect of interest in the decaffeinated coffee abstention comparison. Because our design is balanced, $p = q = 0.5$. Thus, for a 5% one-tailed test with 90% power,

$$^{\delta}R \text{ vs. } A = {}^{\delta}D \text{ vs. } A = 3.5/7 = .5$$

$$^{\Delta}R \text{ vs. } A = {}^{\Delta}D \text{ vs. } A = .5 \Big/ \left[.5^2 + \frac{1}{(.5)(.5)} \right]^{1/2} = .24$$

^{n}R vs. A $= {}^{n}D$ vs. A $= 144 + 2 = 146$, or approximately 73 per group.

In the comparison of decaffeinated and regular coffee, however, the effect of interest is subtler, because we wish to make a much more definitive claim about the hazards associated specifically with caffeine in coffee. If decaffeinated coffee appears to affect health as much as regular coffee does, we would make no strong public policy recommendations concerning it. If, on the other hand, decaffeinated coffee is even slightly less dangerous than regular coffee, we would recommend that both coffee producers and consumers switch to decaffeinated coffee. We therefore decide to investigate effects as subtle as a 1.5-point difference in the CMI scores of regular and decaffeinated coffee drinkers. Here, for a 5% one-tailed test with 90% power,

$$^{\delta}R \text{ vs. } D = 1.5/7 = .21$$

$$^{\Delta}R \text{ vs. } D = .21 \Big/ \left[.21^2 + \frac{1}{(.5)(.5)} \right]^{1/2} = .10$$

^{n}R vs. D $= 852 + 2 = 854$, or approximately 427 per group.

The maximal cell size is therefore approximately 427, and with three groups (regular, decaffeinated, and abstainers), the total sample size for the study is (3)(427) = 1,281.

Just as unwary researchers are likely to ask for 99% power for an effect size of 0.1, and be shocked at the necessity of 150,000 or more subjects to achieve those rather idealistic aims, so are many likely to want to "control for," "block for," "stratify on," or "match for" age, sex, education, IQ, family income, height, weight, family health history, etc., a long list of factors, each measured at several levels. This is done not because it is absolutely necessary to do so, but "just to be on the safe side." Since the total sample size necessary increases more or less proportionately to the number of cells, the price of such a "safety measure" is frequently to increase sample size by a factor or 5 or 10 or more. Instead of requiring 50 subjects, one might well require 500!

Furthermore, such an idealistic list of factors may include education, IQ, family income, race, and other such highly correlated factors. A balanced ANOVA with, for example, IQ and education as factors, may require an equal number of low-IQ subjects with a graduate-level education and high-IQ subjects with a graduate-level education. To find such subjects may not be impossible, but will be very difficult. Not only does increasing the number of factors increase the sample size, but the logistic difficulty of finding such a sample size may be increased as well.

If the factors selected for blocking, stratification, or matching in an ANOVA are carefully chosen to be very highly correlated with the response measure, then, as in the repeated measures design versus the endpoint design in Table 4.4, the δ will increase, the number of subjects per cell will decrease, and despite the fact that there are more cells, the total number of subjects required may also decrease. If the factors are uncorrelated or only moderately correlated with the response, the number of subjects per cell will not decrease, and then, multiplied over the number of cells, the total number of subjects required will increase.

The message is a simple but sometimes uncomfortable one. Careful selection of which factors to include and which to exclude is crucial to successful and cost-effective study design. Only factors that are absolutely *necessary* to the research question, or that have a *documented* and *strong* relationship to the response, should be chosen, and these factors should be relatively *independent* of each other (to avoid problems of confounding or collinearity). Careful choice of a few such factors will increase the power of the design and the scope of the potential findings and lend greater credibility to the validity of the findings. Including marginally relevant factors decreases the power of the design, necessitating a much larger sample size or a greater risk of a "hung jury" (a nonsignificant result) and frequently complicates the implementation of the study as well.

CHAPTER
5

Correlation
Coefficients

In the last chapter, we considered tests of the equality of means. Frequently, however, research questions concern the *association* of variables, rather than simply their means in one or more groups. For instance, rather than testing whether the mean CMI of coffee drinkers is higher than that of abstainers, we could ask whether coffee consumption, measured in cups per day, shows a positive association with CMI response. With this model, someone drinking six cups of coffee per day would be expected to have a higher CMI than someone drinking three cups, who in turn would have a higher CMI than someone who did not drink coffee at all.

Such questions, involving the relationship of two variables, are usually tested with a correlation coefficient.

5.1 Intraclass Correlation Coefficient

If two variables, X and Y, are drawn from a bivariate normal distribution, both with the same variance, their association can be tested with an intraclass correlation coefficient. For instance, we might question whether a self-report measure of health, such as the CMI, provides information comparable to that obtained by a physician interviewing the subject and scoring the same questionnaire. This would be important if we proposed to use self-report CMI as the response in our study.

In this case, we wish to demonstrate that the two scores correlate well, so our null hypothesis is not one of *no* correlation (H_0: $\rho_0 = 0$), but rather one of some minimal association, say H_0: $\rho_0 = 0.5$. How many subjects are required to reject H_0: $\rho_0 = 0.5$ at the 5% level of significance with 90% power?

In this case,

$$\Delta = (\rho - \rho_0)/(1 - \rho\rho_0),$$

$$n = \nu + 1,$$

where ρ is an estimate of the correlation we feel is important to find and ρ_0 is the value specified in the null hypothesis.

Suppose we felt that a correlation coefficient of 0.8 between physician-interview and self-report CMI scores would be considered evidence of excellent agreement. Then

$$\Delta = (0.8 - 0.5)/[1 - (0.8)\,(0.5)] = 0.5$$

For a one-tailed 5% test, with 90% power, ν is 30. Since n = ν + 1, approximately 31 subjects are required for 90% power.

5.2 Product-Moment Correlation Coefficient

As always, the validity of a test depends on whether the data meet the assumptions of that test. The intraclass correlation coefficient is based on the assumption that the two scores come from a bivariate normal distribution and have the same variance. The familiar Pearson product-moment correlation also assumes an underlying bivariate normal distribution, but makes no such assumption about equality of variance. In this case,

$$\Delta = (\rho - \rho_0)/(1 - \rho\rho_0) \tag{5.2}$$

$$n = \nu + 2.$$

If we wished to correlate physician-interview and self-report CMI scores as before, but we suspect that physician scores might show less variability than self-report scores, we would find that for 90% power using a one-tailed 5% test:

$$\Delta = (0.8 - 0.5)/\,[1 - (0.8)\,(0.5)] = 0.5$$

$$n = \nu + 2 = 30 + 2 = 32.$$

In other words, for the price of a single additional subject, a research project can be protected against a possibly unwarranted assumption of equal variances. As in the case of using a t-test rather than a z-test, this seems a trivial price to pay.

The product-moment correlation can also be used when the two scores come from entirely different scales, as long as the essential assumptions are satisfied. We might, for instance, decide to correlate coffee consumption, measured in cups per day, with CMI score. In this case, our null hypothesis is H_0: $\rho_0 = 0$. We use the correlation coefficient considered important, say $\rho = 0.4$, as the effect size in our power calculations. Here, for 90% power (one-tailed 5% test),

$$\Delta = (0.4 - 0)/1 - (0.4)(0)) = 0.4,$$

$$n = \nu + 2 = 49 + 2 = 51.$$

5.3. Rank Correlation Coefficients

Until now, every test we have discussed assumed that the scores were sampled from an underlying normal distribution. In addition, the intraclass and product-moment correlations require that the relationship between the two variables is linear and that the variance of one is the same for any value of the other you might specify (homoscedasticity).

Fortunately, not all these assumptions are crucial to the validity of the tests. The two-sample t-test, for instance, is fairly robust to deviations from normality, as long as the variances in the two groups are comparable (Scheffe, 1959). Similarly, the product-moment correlation is fairly robust with respect to the assumption of normality, but is quite sensitive to violations of the linearity or equal variance assumptions (Kraemer, 1980).

Scores in the real world often fail to satisfy the assumptions of univariate normality, much less those of bivariate or multivariate normality. Coffee consumption, for instance, has a highly skewed distribution, with the vast majority of the population drinking fewer than five cups per day, but a few individuals drinking 10 or 12. Furthermore, the variance of CMI scores is liable to be much greater for the very heavy coffee drinkers than for those with more moderate coffee consumption. In such situations, statisticians frequently recommend the use of *nonparametric tests*, tests that make very few assumptions about the underlying distribution of the scores.

Thus, if we wished to correlate coffee consumption with the CMI, we might prefer to use a nonparametric correlation coefficient, such as Kendall's tau or the Spearman rank correlation (Fieller et al., 1957; Fieller and Pearson, 1961). As above, we consider a correlation of 0.4 to be an effect worth detecting, and we wish to determine the sample size required to test H_0: $\rho_0 = 0$ with 90% power at the 5% level.

For the Spearman rank correlation coefficient,

$$\Delta = (6/\pi) \left[\arcsin (\rho/2) - \arcsin (\rho_0/2) \right], \qquad (5.3.1)$$

$$n = 1.06\, \nu + 3$$

For Kendall's tau,

$$\Delta = (2/\pi) \left[\arcsin (\rho) - \arcsin (\rho_0) \right], \qquad (5.3.2)$$

$$n = 0.437\, \nu + 4.$$

Hence, for a one-tailed test at the 5% level with 90% power in our example of coffee consumption and the CMI, where $\rho = 0.4$ and $\rho_0 = 0$, we find $\Delta = 0.38$ and n = 62 for the Spearman, and $\Delta = 0.26$ and n = 58 for the Kendall. If the product-moment correlation coefficient were appropriate, we would have $\Delta = 0.40$ with n = 51.

TABLE 5
Δ and n* for Product-Moment Correlation, Spearman Rank,
Correlation and Kendall's Tau

δ	Product-Moment		Spearman		Kendall	
	Δ	$n = v + 2$	Δ	$n = 1.06v + 3$	Δ	$n = 0.437v + 4$
0.2	0.2	212	0.19	250	0.13	224
0.3	0.3	93	0.29	107	0.19	106
0.4	0.4	51	0.38	62	0.26	58
0.5	0.5	32	0.48	39	0.33	37
0.6	0.6	21	0.58	26	0.41	25
0.7	0.7	15	0.68	19	0.49	18
0.8	0.8	<10	0.79	<14	0.59	13

*n required for 90% power at the 5% significance level, one-tailed test.

Table 5 shows Δ's and corresponding sample sizes for different ρ's. In every case, nonparametric correlations require a larger sample size than the product-moment correlation, but for correlations of moderate size, the difference is minimal. Once again, recruiting a few extra subjects is generally a small price to pay to ensure the validity of a study's results. If the parametric assumptions were justified, a point that is often open to question, the researcher will have expended a bit of unnecessary time, effort, and money. But if the assumptions on which the parametric test is based were not in fact met, the study will be saved from possibly erroneous conclusions.

CHAPTER
6

Linear Regression

When the research hypothesis concerns the association of two measures, two approaches are possible. The first, discussed in Chapter 5, assumes that both measures are free to vary, and we have simply drawn a random sample from the population of interest to estimate their correlation. The second, discussed here, considers one measure, the "independent" or "predictor" variable, fixed, while the other, the "dependent" or "outcome" variable, is some function of the first which varies. To test such a model, we might simply draw a random sample from the population of interest, or we might sample subjects with specified values of the predictor variable and measure their scores on the outcome variable. We here consider the advantages of the different approaches.

6.1 Choosing the X Values

Suppose, for example, we hypothesized that a subject's CMI is a linear function of his coffee consumption. For convenience, symbolize CMI as "Y" and coffee consumption as "X." We assume, for each subject i, that

$$Y_i = \alpha + \beta X_i + error_i,$$

where the errors are independently normally distributed with mean 0 and variance σ_ϵ^2.

The null hypothesis in this case is that coffee consumption does not improve prediction of CMI, or H_0: $\beta = 0$. Power calculations for the test of this hypothesis are done with

$$\delta = \beta/\sigma_\epsilon \qquad\qquad (6.1)$$

$$\Delta = \delta/(\delta^2 + 1/s_x^2)^{1/2},$$

$$n = \nu + 2,$$

where δ is based on the strength of the relationship and background information and

$$s_x^2 = \Sigma_i (X_i - \bar{X})^2 / n$$

is a design parameter, determined by exactly which X's the researcher chooses to sample.

For instance, the researcher might obtain CMIs only from an equal number of subjects who drank no coffee at all $(X = 0)$ and of those who drank 9 cups per day $(X = 9)$; or from an equal number of subjects who drank no coffee, 1 cup per day, 2 cups, 3, 4, 5, etc., up to 9; or only from subjects who drank 3, 4, 5, or 6 cups per day, obtaining an equal number at each of these fixed X values. These decisions about the spacing of the X's have considerable impact on the power of the design, because s_x^2 ranges from $s_x^2 = 20.25$ when all the observations are taken at $X = 0$ and $X = 9$ to $s_x^2 = 1.25$ when all the observations are between $X = 3$ and $X = 6$.

Table 6.1b shows the Δ's for these three designs for values of δ ranging from 0.1 to 1. In every case, the Δ's when half the observations are taken from each end of the scale are maximal, while the Δ's based on X's sampled only from the middle of the scale are the smallest, and those based on sampling all the X's are intermediate. Thus, a one-tailed test at the 5% level with 90% power and $\delta = 0.3$ would require fewer than 10 subjects if the observations were taken only at $X = 0$ and $X = 9$, but 81 subjects if the observations were spread evenly between $X = 3$ and $X = 6$, and 18 subjects if the observations were spread evenly between $X = 0$ and $X = 9$.

But once again, simply choosing the design with the greatest statistical power is not always the wisest strategy, because power may be gained at the cost of credibility. In this case, the model assumes that CMI is a linear function of coffee drinking; but with only two values of coffee drinking (0 and 9

TABLE 6.1a
Proportions of Sample Taken at Each Possible X Value
in Three Different Designs

	$x =$ 0	1	2	3	4	5	6	7	8	9	s_x^2
Design 1	.5	—	—	—	—	—	—	—	—	.5	20.25
Design 2	.1	.1	.1	.1	.1	.1	.1	.1	.1	.1	8.25
Design 3	—	—	—	.25	.25	.25	.25	—	—	—	1.25

cups per day), it would be impossible to demonstrate the validity of this assumption if it were to be questioned.

Sampling only from the middle of the range of possible X (3, 4, 5, 6) values presents a slightly different problem. With this design, we may be able to verify that CMI shows a linear relation to coffee consumption for between 3 and 6 cups of coffee per day, but we have no way of generalizing beyond these values, to either lesser or greater amounts of coffee. Only by sampling the full range of X values of interest can we draw general conclusions. Furthermore, the wider the range of X values sampled, the larger s_x^2, and hence the larger the Δ.

6.2 Regression Versus Correlation

If, instead of sampling certain fixed X values, the researcher chooses to draw a random sample from a bivariate normal population, then either the regression or the correlation approaches can be applied. Which approach has more power? Neither does, of course: both have the same power.

Recall that for the H_0: $\rho_0 = 0$, $\Delta = \rho$ and $n = \nu + 2$ for the product-moment correlation. If we have randomly sampled a bivariate normal population, then, in the regression model

$$\beta = \rho\sigma_y/\sigma_x, \; \sigma_\epsilon = \sigma_y(1-\rho^2)^{1/2}, \; \text{and} \; E(s_x^2) = \sigma_x^2.$$

When we substitute these values in the formula for Δ in regression, we find

$$\delta = \beta/\sigma_\epsilon = (\rho\sigma_y/\sigma_x)/[\sigma_y(1-\rho^2)^{1/2}] = \rho/[\sigma_x(1-\rho^2)^{1/2}].$$

Then

$$\Delta = \delta/(\delta^2 + 1/s_x^2)^{1/2} \approx \delta/(\delta^2 + 1/\sigma_x^2) = \rho$$

Because $n = \nu + 2$ for regression as well, we see that in this situation, the regression and correlation models have exactly equal critical effect sizes and thus equal necessary sample sizes.

As always, both the research design and the assumptions we are willing to make determine the conclusions we are entitled to draw. The regression model makes no assumptions

TABLE 6.1b
Δ for Different Fixed X Values in Linear Regression*

$\delta = \beta/\sigma_\epsilon$	Design 1	Design 2	Design 3
0.1	0.41	0.28	0.11
0.2	0.67	0.50	0.22
0.3	0.80	0.65	0.32
0.4	0.87	0.75	0.41
0.5	0.91	0.82	0.49
0.6	0.94	0.86	0.56
0.7	0.95	0.90	0.62
0.8	0.96	0.92	0.67
0.9	0.97	0.93	0.71
1.0	0.98	0.94	0.75

*In all cases, an equal number of observations are taken at each X value sampled.

about the distribution of the X's. With judicious choice and allocation of X-values, one can obtain increased power without increasing sample size. If the sample of X-values is not randomly drawn, however, we cannot draw any conclusions about the correlation coefficient between X and Y in the general population, because we will have no information at all about σ_x, and

$$\rho = \beta \sigma_x / \sigma_y, \text{ not } \beta s_x / \sigma_y.$$

6.3. Multiple Linear Regression

Often a researcher decides to investigate the effect of more than one predictor variable on the outcome measure. In this case, the regression model assumes that for each subject i:

$$Y_i = \alpha + \beta_1 X_{i1} + \beta_2 X_{i2} + \ldots + \beta_p X_{ip} + error_i$$

where $X_1, X_2, \ldots X_p$ are the p fixed predictor variables and the errors are independently normally distributed with mean 0 and variance σ_ϵ^2.

To test the effect of any given predictor variable X_j (H_0: $\beta_j = 0$), a t-test is used with $N - p - 1$ degrees of freedom. For this test:

$$\delta = \beta_j / \sigma_\epsilon, \qquad\qquad (6.3)$$

$$n = \nu + p + 1,$$

$$\Delta = \delta / (\delta^2 + 1/w_j^2)^{1/2}.$$

Here w_j^2 depends on the variance of X_j and its correlation with the other predictor variables. The smaller the variance of X_j or the higher its correlation with other predictor variables or combinations of them (collinearity), the smaller the w_j^2 and the larger the sample size necessary for adequate power.

For this reason, researchers should select their predictor variables carefully. Inclusion of a great many (p large) or of any that are closely related to each other will decrease the power to detect any effects at all, or necessitate greatly increased sample size. For example, a researcher might plan to include race, socioeconomic status, level of education, and family income as predictor variables, even if the population studied is 90% white and predominantly middle-class. All four of these measures tend to intercorrelate highly. Detecting a relationship between the outcome variable and a single one of these variables may require 20-50 subjects, but investigating all simultaneously may require 200-500 subjects. The situation vis-à-vis Multiple Linear Regression is very similar to that of balanced ANOVA, as theoretically it must be, and the message is the same: Choose a few predictor variables and choose them carefully.

Homogeneity of
Variance Tests

Just as researchers might wish to estimate the mean of a variable in some specific population, so too might they be interested in the variance. Often a condition or treatment will not systematically affect the means of the variables of interest, but subjects will differ widely in their response, causing an increase in variance. Or, quite commonly, two measures of the same quantity will have essentially the same mean, but one will show much greater variance. This chapter discusses tests appropriate for such situations.

7.1 Two Independent Samples

Suppose that, with a total sample size of n, we sample a proportion p from one population and a proportion q from another (p + q = 1) and measure a variable known to be normally distributed in both populations. To test whether the variance of the first sample (σ_x^2) is greater than that of the second sample (σ_y^2), we compare the ratio of the variances with the F-value at np − 1 and nq − 1 degrees of freedom. Here

$$\Delta = (\sigma_x^2 - \sigma_y^2)/(\sigma_x^2 + \sigma_y^2) \tag{7.1}$$

$$n = [(\nu + 3) + [(\nu + 3)^2 - 16pq(\nu + 2)]^{1/2}]/4pq$$

For instance, even though physician-interview and self-report CMI scores do not differ in terms of their means, one method may yield scores with much smaller variance than the other. In such a situation, we would prefer the score with smaller variance, because the power of a test is always decreased by increased within-group variance.

For example, in the two-sample t-test, with p = q = 0.5,

$$\Delta = \delta/(\delta^2 + 4)^{1/2} \text{ and } n = \nu + 2,$$

where δ is the difference between the two means divided by the pooled within-group standard deviation. Now, if the variance were doubled, δ would decrease by a factor of $2^{1/2}$, and we would have, in terms of the original δ,

$$\Delta = \delta / (\delta^2 + 8)^{1/2}.$$

This means, for example, that doubling the variance would decrease Δ from 0.45 to 0.33 for $\delta = 1$. Thus, instead of 40 subjects, a one-tailed test at the 5% level with 90% power would require approximately 77 subjects. Choosing the measure with the smaller variance, in other words, cuts the necessary sample size for a t-test almost in half.

With these facts in mind, we might design a small study to compare the variances of physician-interview and self-report CMI scores, sampling a total of n subjects, but obtaining scores for a proportion p by self-report and for the remaining proportion q by physician interview. The standard deviation of the self-report scores is known to be approximately 6 ($\sigma_x = 6$) from previous work, so the variance is approximately 36 ($\sigma_x^2 = 36$). If the variance of the x physician-interview scores were half that, or approximately 18 ($\sigma_y^2 = 18$), we would consider using these in future studies, even though they are substantially more expensive to obtain. Thus,

$$\Delta = (\sigma_x^2 - \sigma_y^2) / (\sigma_x^2 + \sigma_y^2) = (36 - 18) / (36 + 18) = 0.33$$

The important design decision in this study, just as with the two-sample t-test, is the choice of the proportions p and q. When $p = q = 0.5$, the formula for n simplifies to:

$$n = 2\nu + 4$$

Thus, for 90% power at the 5% level

$$n = 2(75) + 4 = 154$$

When $p = 0.9$ and $q = 0.1$, on the other hand, calculations yield

$$n = \frac{(75 + 3) + [(75 + 3)^2 - 16(0.9)\,(0.1)\,(75 + 2)]^{1/2}}{4(0.9)\,(0.1)} \approx 432$$

Table 7.1 gives more information on the effect of imbalance on necessary sample size for selected values of ν and p. As in the case of t-tests, mild imbalance has little impact, but extremely imbalanced groups ($p, q \geq 0.75$) will require significantly more subjects than a balanced design to achieve the same power. As with the t-test, power is maximized, and therefore sample size is minimized at $p = 0.5$.

7.2 Matched Samples

Rather than using two independent samples to test the hypothesis that self-report and physician-interview CMI scores have the same variance (cross-sectional study), we might choose to study one set of subjects under both conditions, using the same sort of repeated-measures design we used for the matched-pairs t-test. The test in this case, developed by Morgan (1939) and Pitman (1939), has:

$$\Delta = (\sigma_x^2 - \sigma_y^2)/[(\sigma_x^2 + \sigma_y^2)^2 - 4\rho^2\,\sigma_x^2\,\sigma_y^2]^{1/2} \qquad (7.2)$$

$$n = \nu + 2$$

where σ_x^2 is the variance of the first measure, σ_y^2 that of the second and ρ the corrrelation between the two (Kraemer, 1981).

To continue the example above, suppose the correlation between physician-interview and self-report scores were 0.5 ($\rho = .5$), and the variance of the physician scores is still 18

TABLE 7.1
Sample Sizes for Varying Degrees of Imbalance
in the Two-Group Variance-Ratio Test

ν	0.5	0.6, 0.4	0.7, 0.3	0.8, 0.2	0.9, 0.1
			$p, q =$		
20	44	46	53	70	126
30	64	67	77	102	182
40	84	88	101	133	237
50	104	109	125	164	293
60	124	130	148	195	349
70	144	151	172	227	404
80	164	171	196	258	460
90	184	192	220	289	515
100	204	213	244	320	571

($\sigma_y^2 = 18$), while that of the self-report scores is 36 ($\sigma_x^2 = 36$). Then

$$\Delta = (36 - 18)/[(36 + 18)^2 - (4)(0.5)^2(36)(18)]^{1/2} = 0.38,$$

$$n = 55 + 2 = 57$$

for 90% power at the 5% significance level. Here, we require 57 subjects each measured twice (114 observations) rather than 154 subjects each measured once (154 observations), when we proposed to use independent (unmatched) groups and a balanced design.

The power of the matched design increases with the degree of correlation between paired responses (ρ). Table 7.2 shows the effect on Δ of an increasing correlation coefficient between the two scores. When the correlation is 0, the scores are independent, and this design is equivalent to the two-group (unmatched) design with equal group sizes, except that only

TABLE 7.2
Values of Δ for Differing Values of the Variance Ratio (σ_x^2/σ_y^2) and Correlation (ρ) Between Responses in the Matched Sample Test

(σ_x^2/σ_y^2)	$\rho =$ 0.00	0.1	0.2	0.3	0.4	0.5	0.6	0.7	0.8	0.9
1.00	0.00	0.00	0.00	0.00	0.00	0.00	0.00	0.00	0.00	0.00
1.25	0.11	0.11	0.11	0.12	0.12	0.13	0.14	0.15	0.18	0.25
1.50	0.20	0.20	0.20	0.21	0.22	0.23	0.25	0.27	0.32	0.42
2.00	0.33	0.33	0.34	0.35	0.36	0.38	0.40	0.44	0.51	0.63
2.50	0.43	0.43	0.44	0.45	0.46	0.48	0.51	0.55	0.62	0.74
3.00	0.50	0.50	0.51	0.52	0.53	0.55	0.59	0.63	0.69	0.80
4.00	0.60	0.60	0.61	0.62	0.63	0.65	0.68	0.72	0.78	0.86
6.00	0.71	0.72	0.72	0.73	0.74	0.76	0.79	0.82	0.86	0.92
9.00	0.80	0.80	0.81	0.81	0.82	0.84	0.86	0.88	0.91	0.95
20.00	0.90	0.91	0.91	0.91	0.92	0.93	0.94	0.95	0.96	0.98
100.00	0.98	0.98	0.98	0.98	0.98	0.99	0.99	0.99	0.99	1.00

half as many subjects (ν + 2 rather than 2ν + 4) are required, because each subject is measured twice. If recruiting subjects is difficult, then feasibility considerations alone will argue for a matched design. If the correlation between the scores is even moderately strong, then the matched design offers significantly more power as well, and in such situations, the Morgan-Pitman test statistic will generally be preferred to the more familiar variance-ratio F-test.

CHAPTER
8

Binomial Tests

All the tests discussed thus far have been based on measurements that can at least be ordered. In fact, except for nonparametric correlation, we have assumed not only ordinal measures, but also that the underlying distributions were in some way normal. Research, however, often concerns nominal level variables, variables resulting from categories that cannot even be ordered, far less considered normally distributed. Gender, race, and religious affiliation are examples of such variables. This chapter discusses tests appropriate for dichotomous variables, like gender, with only two values.

8.1 Single-Sample Binomial Tests

Because dichotomous variables can assume only two values, questions about them concern not their means, but the proportion of the sample assuming each value. Just as the one-sample t-test can be used either to compare the mean of a single measurement with some specified value, or to detect a difference between the means of paired scores (matched-pairs t-test), so can the one-sample binomial be used either to compare the proportions in a sample with some specified value (usually 0.5) or to detect a difference in paired values.

For convenience, call the two values of the variable "Yes" and "No," and let π be the proportion of "Yes" responses we consider it important to detect, while π_0 is the proportion specified under the null hypothesis. Then, to use the Master Table:

$$\delta = 2\,(\arcsin \pi^{1/2} - \arcsin \pi_0^{1/2}), \qquad (8.1.1)$$

$$\Delta = (e^{2\delta} - 1)/(e^{2\delta} + 1),$$

$$n = \nu - 1.$$

Suppose, for example, that instead of some scaled measure of health like the CMI, we had only information about whether the subject sought medical treatment (other than a routine physical) in the past year (Yes) or not (No). We wish to discover whether the proportion of those seeking treatment was higher among coffee drinkers than in the general population. Suppose we decide to sample coffee drinkers in their fifties, reasoning that their exposure to coffee has been sufficient to affect their health, and wish to detect an increase of 10% in the proportion seeking medical care with 90% power at the 5% level of significance. If the proportion of the general population in their fifties seeking medical treatment is known to be 0.5 ($\pi_0 = 0.5$) then for a 10% increase ($\pi = .6$):

$$\delta = 2\,(\arcsin 0.6^{1/2} - \arcsin 0.5^{1/2}) = 0.20,$$

$$\Delta = (e^{2\delta} - 1)/(e^{2\delta} + 1) = 0.20,$$

$$n = \nu - 1 = 209.$$

There are several versions of this test in common use under different names. The equivalent of the matched-pairs t-test for a dichotomous (Yes/No) variable is called McNemar's test (Siegel, 1956). In this test, all tied pairs (i.e., Yes-Yes or No-No) are discarded, and a single-sample binomial is used to test whether the proportion of Yes-No pairs equals the proportion of No-Yes pairs (i.e., $\pi_0 = .5$). Here π is the Yes-No proportion among untied pairs and γ the proportion of untied pairs. Then:

$$\delta = 2\,[(\arcsin \pi^{1/2} - \arcsin 0.5^{1/2})], \qquad (8.1.2)$$

$$\Delta = (e^{2\delta} - 1)/(e^{2\delta} + 1),$$

$$n = (\nu - 1)/\gamma.$$

If half the subjects are expected to give the same response both times ($\gamma = 0.50$), in other words, then $2(\nu - 1)$ subjects must be

sampled to achieve the specified power, while if 75% respond
the same way both times (γ = 0.25), then n = 4(v – 1). Thus,
McNemar's test can require extremely large sample sizes if
used with highly correlated responses that produce small
values of γ.

The sign test (Siegel, 1956) and the single-sample
median test are also special applications of the single-sample
binomial test, in which observations are dichotomized as
"Yes" or "No" according to whether they satisfy some ordering
or not. For instance, in the single-sample median test, scores
may be dichotomized as to whether they fall above or below a
median specified in the null hypothesis.

Suppose, for example, we wished to test whether the
mean μ of some normally distributed variable with variance σ^2
were in fact 0. Since the mean equals the median in a normal
distribution, we could either use the single-sample t-test, or we
could dichotomize the data, denoting all positive values as
"Yes" and all negative values as "No," and testing whether
there were approximately equal numbers of positive and negative scores (π_0 = 0.5) with the single-sample binomial test.
Recall that for the one-sample t-test (4.1):

$$\delta = \mu/\sigma,$$
$$\Delta = \delta/(\delta^2 + 1)^{1/2},$$
$$n = \nu + 1.$$

For the binomial test (8.1) in this situation we have:

$$\pi = \Phi(\mu/\sigma) = \Phi(\delta)$$

where Φ is the cumulative standard normal distribution function, and

$$\delta = 2\,[\arcsin \pi^{1/2} - \arcsin 0.5^{1/2}],$$

$$\Delta = (e^{2\delta} - 1)/(e^{2\delta} + 1),$$

$$n = \nu - 1.$$

Table 8.1 shows the relationship of π to $\delta = \mu/\sigma$ and the corresponding Δ's for the binomial and t-tests. In every case, the Δ for the binomial test is smaller than that for the t-test: More subjects would be required to achieve the same power. For instance, if $\delta = 0.1$, for a one-tailed test at the 5% level with 90% power, we have, for the t-test:

$$\Delta = 0.10,$$

$$n = 852 + 1 = 853,$$

and for the binomial,

$$\Delta = 0.08,$$

$$n = 1334 - 1 = 1333,$$

a difference of almost 500 subjects. How the response is measured, whether on a continuum or dichotomized, can make a significant difference in the power of the test. The researcher must consider whether the greater ease of using a dichotomy instead of a continuous variable outweighs the effort and expense of studying this many more subjects (Cohen, 1983).

8.2 Two-Sample Binomial Test

Like the t-test, the binomial can be used both to compare the scores of one sample to some specified value as discussed above, or to compare the scores of two samples with

TABLE 8.1
Comparison of Δ for Single-Sample t-test
and Single-Sample Binomial

$\delta = \mu/\sigma$	π^*	Δ for t	Δ for binomial
0.1	0.54	0.10	0.08
0.2	0.58	0.20	0.16
0.3	0.62	0.29	0.23
0.4	0.66	0.37	0.31
0.5	0.69	0.45	0.37
0.6	0.73	0.51	0.44
0.7	0.76	0.57	0.49
0.8	0.79	0.62	0.55
0.9	0.82	0.67	0.59
1.0	0.84	0.71	0.64

$^*\pi = \Phi(\delta)$ where Φ is the cumulative standard normal distribution function.

each other. In the two-sample case, if the total sample size is n, and we sample a fraction p from one group and a fraction q from a second (p + q = 1), then, to use the Master Table,

$$\delta = 2\,(pq)^{1/2}\,(\arcsin \pi_x^{1/2} - \arcsin \pi_y^{1/2}), \qquad (8.2)$$

$$\Delta = (e^{2\delta} - 1)/(e^{2\delta} + 1),$$

$$n = \nu - 1,$$

where π_x and π_y are the proportions of "Yes" response in the two groups.

Suppose, for example, that instead of comparing the proportion of coffee drinkers in their fifties seeking medical care to that of the hypothetical general population, we chose to compare coffee drinkers with abstainers, again using a 10% difference as the effect we wish to detect with 90% power at the 5% significance level. As with the two-sample t-test and the independent-group variance ratio test, power is maximized with a balanced (p = q = 0.5) design, and will be severely diminished with very unbalanced (p $\geq$ 0.75, roughly) group sizes. We therefore choose p = q = 0.5, and use as our estimate of π_y (the proportion of coffee abstainers seeking medical care) the proportion of the general population of subjects in their fifties who seek medical care, known from previous studies to be about 0.5 (π_y = .5). Hence for a 10% increase (π_x = .6):

$$\delta = 2\,((0.5)\,(0.5))^{1/2}\,[(\arcsin 0.6^{1/2} - \arcsin 0.5^{1/2})] = 0.1$$

$$\Delta = (e^{0.2} - 1)/(e^{0.2} + 1) = 0.1$$

$$n = \nu - 1 = 852 - 1 = 851,$$

meaning approximately 426 subjects per group are required for 90% power.

As noted above, researchers sometimes choose to dichotomize a continuous variable. In such a situation, a two-sample binomial might be used instead of the two-sample t-test. If, for example, a variable is normally distributed with mean μ_x in one group and mean μ_y in the second group, both having a common variance σ^2, then the t-test could be used with

$$\delta = (\mu_x - \mu_y)/\sigma$$

$$\Delta = \delta/(\delta^2 + 1/pq)^{1/2},$$

$$n = \nu + 2.$$

On the other hand, if the variable were dichotomized at point $\bar{\mu} + C\sigma$, where the $\bar{\mu}$ is the average of the two group means, then:

$$\pi_x = \Phi\,(C + \delta/2), \quad \pi_y = \Phi\,(C - \delta/2),$$

and the two-sample binomial could be used with:

$$\delta = 2\,(pq)^{1/2}\,[\arcsin \pi_x^{1/2} - \arcsin \pi_y^{1/2}],$$

$$\Delta = (e^{2\delta} - 1)/(e^{2\delta} + 1),$$

$$n = \nu - 1.$$

Table 8.2.1 shows the effect of varying the cut-off value (C) for different values of $\delta = (\mu_x - \mu_y)/\sigma$. In every case, the critical effect size for the binomial test is smaller than that for the t-test. When the cut-off is halfway between the two group means (C = 0), the effect size is largest, but even then there is some loss.

How serious the problems can be is better seen in Table 8.2.2, where the example considered in Chapter 4 for the two-sample t-test is reconsidered. In that example, we saw that when $\delta = .5$, and seeking 80% power for a 5% one-tailed test, we needed 107 subjects for a balanced or near-balanced design, but as many as 274 subjects with a 90-10 split in group sizes (see

TABLE 8.2.1
Critical Effect Sizes (Δ) for a Balanced Two-Sample t-test
and Binomial Test with Different Points of Dichotomization

	Binomial Test					t-test
δ	C: ±2	± 1.5	± 1	± 0.5	0	Δ for t
0.1	0.02	0.03	0.03	0.04	0.04	0.05
0.2	0.04	0.05	0.07	0.08	0.08	0.10
0.3	0.05	0.08	0.10	0.11	0.12	0.15
0.4	0.07	0.10	0.13	0.15	0.16	0.20
0.5	0.09	0.13	0.16	0.19	0.20	0.24
0.6	0.11	0.15	0.20	0.22	0.23	0.29
0.7	0.13	0.18	0.23	0.26	0.27	0.33
0.8	0.14	0.20	0.26	0.29	0.31	0.37
0.9	0.16	0.23	0.29	0.33	0.34	0.41
1	0.18	0.25	0.32	0.36	0.37	0.45

TABLE 8.2.2
Sample Size Necessary for 80% Power to Detect $\delta = .5$
Using a One-Tailed 5% Test with the t-test and with the
Binomial Test for Balanced (p, q = .5) and Unbalanced Designs
and Various Cutoffs (C) for Dichotomizing $\delta = .5$ Responses

		Binomial Test				
p, q	t-test	C: 0.0	0.5	1.0	1.5	2.0
0.1	274	426	507	615	962	2469
0.2	154	238	271	362	615	1258
0.3	127	187	210	271	426	962
0.4	107	168	187	238	362	760
0.5	107	151	168	238	362	760

t-test column in Table 8.2.2). As one dichotomizes at various cut-off points (C), the sample size increases to 2469. The discrepancy between 107 and 2469 subjects is far from trivial and should cause a researcher to pause and consider whether the ease of using dichotomous response instead of a continuous response is worth the effort and expense of studying so many more subjects (Cohen, 1983).

Contingency Table Analysis

9.1 Introduction

One of the easiest and most common of statistical tests is the $I \times J$ contingency table χ^2-test. Unfortunately, it is also one of the most difficult tests for which to plan and, in addition, one of the very weakest of tests. For this test, each of a sample of n subjects is classified into categories $X1, X2, \ldots, XI$ and categories $Y1, Y2, \ldots, YJ$, the data summarized in an $I \times J$ table (Table 9.1). To test the association (correlation, dependency) between X and Y, a statistic is computed and referred to the χ^2-table with $(I-1)(J-1)$ degrees of freedom. A number of issues must be considered.

First of all, the test statistic can validly be referred to the χ^2-table only if the sample is large enough to yield a reasonable number in each marginal position (np_i and nq_j). There is no general agreement as to how large is "reasonable." One of the more common rules of thumb is that:

$$np_iq_j \geq 5 \text{ for each i and j.}$$

One or more rare categories (eg., $p_i = 0.05$, $q_j = 0.1$) will necessitate a large minimal sample size (e.g., $n(0.05)(0.1) \geq 5$ means $n \geq 1000$) to use the test at all, even before power is at issue. With an $I \times J$ table, the minimal total sample size under any conditions is therefore 5IJ (i.e., $(5)(3)(4) = 60$ for a 3×4 table).

Second, there are a variety of possible sampling plans. A representative sample of size n may be drawn from some population with responses falling where they may in the $I \times J$ table: *Naturalistic Sampling*. In that case, $p_1, p_2, \ldots, p_i$ and $q_1, q_2 \ldots, q_j$ estimate the probability distributions of X and Y in the population. Alternatively, the researchers may select proportions $p_1, p_2, \ldots, p_i$ in each X-category and let the Y-responses in each row fall where they may: *X-Stratified Sampling*, or they may select proportions $q_1, q_2 \ldots, q_J$ in each

TABLE 9.1
An I × J Contingency Table

	Y1	Y2 ... YJ	
X1			np_1
X2			np_2
XI			np_I
	$n_1,$	$nq_2 \ldots nq_j$	

Y-category and let the X-responses in each column fall where they may: *Y-Stratified Sampling*. In each of the stratified cases the p_i's and q_j's reflect design decisions and cannot be used to estimate population characteristics. Because one can stratify to avoid rare categories, stratified sampling usually yields more power than naturalistic sampling.

Third, this test is designed for use when the X and Y categories are unordered. When either X or Y are ordered, this test remains valid but is far less powerful than other valid nonparametric tests that capitalize on the ordering (rank correlations, Mann-Whitney, Kruskal-Wallis).

What we suggest for power calculation is this: We dissect the full I × J table into IJ 2 × 2 tables. For each pair of X and Y categories, we decide whether or not that particular association is important. If it is important, we decide how strong an association it is critical to detect and base power calculations on that decision.

9.2 The I × J χ^2-test

For each X_i and Y_j whose association we consider important, we reduce the I × J table to a 2 × 2 table (Table 9.2).

In Naturalistic Sampling, p_i and q_j are the probabilities of observing X_i and Y_j; in X-stratified samples p_i is the proportion of the sample the researcher has decided to obtain and q_j the proportion of Y_j that result; and in Y-stratified samples q_j is the proportion of the sample the researcher has decided to obtain and p_i the proportion of X_i that results.

The proportions a, b, c, d are selected to represent the type of association it is critical to detect. To use the χ^2-test at all:

$$n \geqslant 5/\min [p_i q_j, \ p_i(1 - q_j), \ (1 - p_i)q_j, \ (1 - p_i)(1 - q_j)]. \quad (9.2.1)$$

Obviously, rare categories will automatically necessitate a large sample size.

If the sample is X-stratified, the 2×2 χ^2-test is essentially a 2-sample binomial test and:

$$\delta = 2 [p_i(1 - p_i)]^{1/2} [\arcsin (a/p_i)^{1/2}$$
$$- \arcsin (c/ (1 - p_i))^{1/2}] \quad (9.2.2)$$
$$\Delta = (e^{2\delta} - 1)/(e^{2\delta} + 1)$$
$$n = \nu - 1.$$

If the sample is Y-stratified, the situation is similar, and:

$$\delta = 2 [q_j(1 - q_j)]^{1/2} [\arcsin (a/q_j)^{1/2}$$
$$- \arcsin (b/(1 - q_j))^{1/2}] \quad (9.2.3)$$
$$\Delta = (e^{2\delta} - 1)/(e^{2\delta} + 1)$$
$$n = \nu - 1.$$

If the sample is naturalistic, either of the above calculations is applicable. In this case, the results of the two calculations for Δ rarely differ by more than 0.01.

TABLE 9.2
A 2 × 2 Reduced Table

	Y_j	not Y_j	
X_i	a	b	p_i
not X_i	c	d	$1 - p_i$
	q_j	$1 - q_j$	

Whichever n is largest (that from 9.2.1 or that from 9.2.2 or 9.2.3) is the required sample size for that X, Y pair. This process is repeated for each X, Y pair whose association is considered important. The overall recommended sample size is the maximal value of all these sample sizes.

Obviously, sample size must be very large to use a χ^2-test efficiently. The larger the number of categories, or the rarer some of the categories, the larger the sample size. For this reason, we recommend that the χ^2-test be used only when there is no other recourse (i.e., the categories cannot be ordered) and, even then, that the number of categories be limited to those essential to the hypothesis. To use the χ^2-test under other circumstances wastes power and entails unnecessary expense.

9.3 An Example of a 3 × 2 Contingency Table Analyis

Suppose, as in Chapter 8, that we wish to determine the association between coffee consumption and the need for nonroutine medical care for subjects in their fifties, but this time we wish to distinguish between use of regular and decaffeinated

TABLE 9.3a

	Medical care	
	No	Yes
no		
reg or decaf		

	Medical care	
	No	Yes
no or decaf		
reg		

	Medical care	
	No	Yes
no or reg		
decaf		

coffee. The variable "coffee consumption" thus corresponds to three categories (none (no), only decaffeinated (decaf), and regular (reg) coffee) which we do not consider to be ordered. The measure of medical care remains a dichotomy ("yes" or "no"). The resulting 3×2 table can be broken down into three different 2×2 comparisons (Table 9.3a).

The first case corresponds to the hypothesis that coffee use itself is a risk factor, regardless of caffeine content, while the second corresponds to the hypothesis that only coffee with caffeine is associated with an increased need for medical care. The third case, corresponding to the hypothesis that decaffeinated coffee poses risks, while drinking regular coffee is no different from abstaining entirely, we do not consider of interest in the present context, and dismiss it. The necessary sample size is therefore the maximum of that required by the first two cases.

To avoid problems with rare categories (e.g., subjects who drink only decaffeinated coffee), we decide to stratify on coffee consumption, selecting a sample with equal numbers of ordinary coffee drinkers, abstainers, and those who drink only decaffeinated coffee (p_1, p_2, $p_3 \approx 1/3$). As in Chapter 8, we expect that approximately 50% of subjects in their fifties who do not drink coffee at all will seek nonroutine medical care in a given year, and we consider it important to detect a 10% increase in this rate for ordinary coffee drinkers. We expect subjects who drink only decaffeinated coffee to seek care at an intermediate rate. Table 9.3b, a 3×2 table, therefore represents the proportions in the total sample corresponding to the association we consider important to detect. Power calculations are therefore based on the two comparisons of interest (see Table 9.3c).

As before, we wish to detect an association of this type with 90% power at the 5% level of significance.

In the first case:

$$\delta = 2\,[(.34)\,(.66)]^{1/2}\,(\arcsin(.17/.34)^{1/2}$$
$$- \arcsin(.28/.66)^{1/2}] = .07,$$
$$\Delta = (e^{2\delta} - 1)/(e^{2\delta} + 1) = .07,$$
$$n = 1744 - 1 = 1743.$$

In the second case:

$$\delta = 2\,[(.67)\,(.33)]^{1/2}\,(\arcsin(.32/.67)^{1/2}$$
$$- \arcsin(.13/.33)^{1/2} = .08,$$
$$\Delta = (e^{2\delta} - 1)/(e^{2\delta} + 1) = .08,$$
$$n = 1334 - 1 = 1333.$$

The sample size necessary for all comparisons of interest is therefore approximately 1743, or more than twice that required by the binomial test to compare coffee drinkers with abstainers. Expanding the design to include a group of decaffeinated coffee drinkers enables us to answer questions about whether regular coffee poses a greater risk than decaf-

TABLE 9.3b

	Medical care		
	No	Yes	
no coffee	0.17	0.17	0.34
decaffeinated	0.15	0.18	0.33
regular	0.13	0.20	0.33
	0.45	0.55	

TABLE 9.3c

	Medical care		
	No	Yes	
no coffee	0.17	0.17	0.34
regular or decaf	0.28	0.38	0.66
	0.45	0.55	

	Medical care		
	No	Yes	
no or decaf	0.32	0.35	0.67
regular	0.13	0.20	0.33
	0.45	0.55	

feinated or whether drinking decaffeinated coffee differs from abstaining from coffee entirely. However, broadening the hypothesis in this way entails studying many more subjects. As always, the researcher must decide whether the value of the additional information justifies the cost of collecting it.

CHAPTER
10

Conclusions

Obviously, it is not easy to plan successful and cost-effective research projects. Such planning requires a considerable degree of expertise in the field of application, experience, instinct, flexibility, and creativeness. While computing a 2×2 χ^2-test is relatively easy, it is considerably more difficult to decide whether the 2×2 test is the best test to use, what other tests might be appropriate, how many subjects to sample, and how to sample them. Furthermore, making a mistake in calculating a χ^2-test at the end of a study is easily corrected, for one may always redo the test. Making a mistake in planning a study as to what data to collect and how many subjects to study is irrevocable.

This book was written to allow researchers to include explicit power calculations in the planning of their research projects. However, researchers who know how to do statistical analyses do not necessarily do their own analyses, nor do researchers who know how to do power calculations necessarily take on the onus of all such considerations without statistical consultation. The goals of having a general understanding of the concept of power are somewhat broader.

First, researchers would make a clear distinction between preliminary evidence (exploratory data analysis) and the actual "trial by jury" (confirmatory data analysis or hypothesis testing). "Post hoc" testing or "fishing expeditions" using statistical tests as the "hook" would be more strongly discouraged than they are now.

Second, researchers should be encouraged to realize that one does not go to trial until considerable preliminary evidence is in hand, much of it quantitative in nature. Extensive exploratory data analysis and meta-analysis on related issues prior to going to trial are essential to plan effective strategy and to define a critical effect size. Statistical hypothesis testing is often premature, done at a stage when cost-effective planning is not possible.

If this were clearly understood, perhaps journal editors and reviewers would be more receptive to well-done exploratory studies, recognizing that such studies are the necessary prelude to well-planned and well-executed confirmatory studies and are valuable in their own right.

Third, researchers would be encouraged to report the results of studies, both exploratory and confirmatory, in terms of effect sizes. The results of a study should be described in sufficient statistical detail that they can be used in planning any further studies of the same hypothesis or of related issues in the same field. As the statistical procedures underlying meta-analysis are improved (Hedges and Olkin, 1985), presentation of such details will be facilitated. Results should never be reported only in terms of "NS" or one, two, or three asterisks. These are uninformative symbols, giving no specific information as to what is going on.

Finally, researchers would be encouraged to think in terms of cost-efficiency to a much greater extent than they do now.

For example, each measure of response should be used in as sensitive a form as it can be reliably measured. If response can be reliably measured on a continuum, it should not be reduced to a 5-point scale, a 3-point scale, or dichotomized. A measure of response reliably obtainable on a 5-point scale should not be reduced to a 3-point scale or dichotomized. To do so is to lose information, to lose power in all analyses, and consequently to necessitate a much larger sample size to achieve adequate power. The costs of unnecessary dichotomization have been demonstrated in some detail here, and similar demonstrations are possible for 3-, 4-, or 5-point scales derived from a continuum. In all such cases, power depends not merely on how many points but on exactly where the cutoffs between successive scale values are made. It is all too easy to set the cutoffs ineffectively.

One should match, stratify, or block only on factors that are known to affect the response measure quite strongly, that can be very reliably measured, and that are relatively independent of other factors used for matching, stratifying, or blocking. This means, in effect, that one should match, stratify, or block on as few factors as are necessary to validly answer the research question. If factors that are only weakly correlated with outcome, or factors poorly measured, or redundant factors are used, not only is the conduct and execution of the research project made more difficult, but the net result may be a loss of power or vastly increased necessary sample size. We have seen such problems both in ANOVA and Multiple Linear Regression.

One should always choose the most powerful statistical test that is valid for the question and data in hand. If the parametric assumptions are not met, one should use the Wilcoxon Signed Rank test instead of a matched-pairs t-test, the Mann-Whitney test instead of the two-sample t-test, the Kruskal-Wallis test instead of a one-way ANOVA, the Friedman test instead of a two-way ANOVA, the Spearman or Kendall instead of the Pearson correlation coefficient. In all such cases, there is some loss of power, but it is minimal. One might require a few more subjects, but that is a small price to guarantee the validity of the conclusions.

On the other hand, to use a χ^2 contingency table analysis to assess the correlation between two ordinal 5-point scales instead of a nonparametric correlation coefficient may necessitate increasing the sample size by 100-200% (Cohen, 1983). Since the cost of research and the time needed for completion of a project are usually directly related to sample size, such practices expend researchers' own and others' resources needlessly.

Without the necessary tools to think through such problems, specifically without a good grasp of what affects power in statistical testing, researchers find it difficult to make decisions in the most cost-effective fashion. Frequently what seems intuitively obvious is not only not obvious, but not even true.

What is worse, when seeking statistical consultation, such issues of particular and specific relevance in their own fields of research may never be brought to the attention of the consulting statistician. A consulting statistician not versed in psychiatric diagnosis, for example, may not know that there are several extant valid and reliable scales measuring severity of clinical depression. The possibility of using such a scale rather than a depressed/nondepressed dichotomy in a clinical drug trial may simply not arise for discussion. The researcher is then informed that 500 patients might be needed and never realize that 50 might otherwise have sufficed. As a result, the most cost-effective decisions are not necessarily the ones made, even with expert advice.

It is not a minor problem that those who are able to do power calculations readily are generally those who least know the fields of application, and those who best know the fields of application are least able to do power calculations. As a result we feel that the most beneficial effect of a clearer understanding of power considerations is to alert researchers to the kinds and range of issues involved in planning powerful research studies, and to clarify communication among researchers themselves and with their statistical consultants.

SUMMARY TABLE

TEST	SPECIFICATION	H_0	ν	Δ	SECTION
Single-Sample Normal Test	$X_i \sim N(\mu, \sigma^2)$ $i = 1, 2, \ldots, n$ σ^2 known	$\mu = \mu_0$	$n + 1$	$\Delta = (e^{2\delta} - 1)/(e^{2\delta} + 1)$ $\delta = (\mu - \mu_0)/\sigma$	4.1
Single-Sample t Matched Pair t	$X_i \sim N(\mu, \sigma^2)$ $i = 1, 2, \ldots, n$	$\mu = \mu_0$	$n - 1$	$\Delta = \delta/(\delta^2 + 1)^{1/2}$ $\delta = (\mu - \mu_0)/\sigma$	4.2
Two-Sample t	$X_i \sim N(\mu_x, \sigma^2)$ $i = 1, 2, \ldots, np$ $Y_i \sim N(\mu_y, \sigma^2)$ $i = 1, 2, \ldots, nq$ $p + q = 1$	$\mu_x = \mu_y$	$n - 2$	$\Delta = \delta/(\delta^2 + 1/pq)^{1/2}$ $\delta = (\mu_x - \mu_y)/\sigma$	4.3
Intraclass ρ	(x_i, y_i) Bivariate Normal $\text{corr}(X_i, Y_i) = \rho$	$\rho = \rho_0$	$n - 1$	$\Delta = (\rho - \rho_0)/(1 - \rho\rho_0)$	5.1

(continued)

SUMMARY TABLE Continued

TEST	SPECIFICATION	H_0	ν	Δ	SECTION
	$i = 1, 2, \ldots, n$ $\sigma_x^2 = \sigma_y^2$				
Product-Moment ρ	$(x_i y_i)$ Bivariate Normal $\mathrm{corr}(X_i, Y_i) = \rho$ $i = 1, 2, \ldots, n$	$\rho = \rho_0$	$n - 2$	$\Delta = (\rho - \rho_0)/(1 - \rho\rho_0)$	5.2
Spearman ρ	$(x_i y_i)$ Bivariate Normal $\mathrm{corr}(X_i, Y_i) = \rho$ $i = 1, 2, \ldots, n$	$\rho = \rho_0$	$(n - 3)/1.060$	$\Delta = \dfrac{6}{\pi} \left[\arcsin(\rho/2) - \arcsin(\rho_0/2) \right]$	5.3
Kendall ρ	$(x_i y_i)$ Bivariate Normal $\mathrm{corr}(X_i, Y_i) = \rho$ $i = 1, 2, \ldots, n$	$\rho = \rho_0$	$(n - 4)/.437$	$\Delta = \dfrac{2}{\pi} \left[\arcsin(\rho) - \arcsin(\rho_0) \right]$	5.3

	Assumptions	Null Hypothesis	df	Effect Size	
Linear Regression	$Y_i \sim \alpha + \beta X_i + \epsilon_i$ $i = 1, 2, \ldots, n$ $\epsilon_i \sim N(0, \sigma_\epsilon^2)$ X_i regarded as fixed with some variance s_x^2	$\beta = \beta_0$	$n - 2$	$\Delta = \delta/(\delta^2 + 1/s_x^2)^{1/2}$ $\delta = (\beta - \beta_0)/\sigma_\epsilon$	6.1
Variance Ratio Test Independent Samples	$X_i \sim N(\mu_x, \sigma_x^2)$ $1 = 1, 2, \ldots, np$ $Y_i \sim N(\mu_y, \sigma_y^2)$ $1 = 1, 2, \ldots, nq$ $p + 1 = 1$	$\sigma_x^2 = \sigma_y^2$	$\dfrac{(2n^2 pq - 3n + 4)}{(n - 2)}$	$\Delta = (\sigma_x^2 - \sigma_y^2)/(\sigma_x^2 + \sigma_y^2)$	7.1
Variance Ratio Test Matched Samples	(x_i, y_i) Bivariate Normal $\mathrm{corr}(X_i, Y_i) = \rho$ $i = 1, 2, \ldots, n$	$\sigma_x^2 = \sigma_y^2$	$n - 2$	$\Delta = (\sigma_x^2 - \sigma_y^2)/[(\sigma_x^2 + \sigma_y^2)^2 - 4\rho^2 \sigma_x^2 \sigma_y^2]^{1/2}$	7.2

(continued)

103

SUMMARY TABLE Continued

TEST	SPECIFICATION	H_0	ν	Δ	SECTION
Sign, Median, or Single Sample Binomial	$X_i \sim B(n, \pi)$ $i = 1, 2, \ldots, n$	$\pi = \pi_0$	$n + 1$	$\Delta = (e^{2\delta} - 1)/(e^{2\delta} + 1)$ $\delta = 2[\arcsin \pi^{1/2} - \arcsin \pi_0^{1/2}]$	8.1
Two-Sample Binomial Test (2×2 χ^2 Stratified)	$X_i \sim B(\pi_x)$ $i = 1, 2, \ldots, np$ $Y_i \sim B(\pi_y)$ $i = 1, 2, \ldots, nq$ $p + q = 1$	$\pi_x = \pi_y$	$n + 1$	$\Delta = (e^{2\delta} - 1)/(e^{2\delta} + 1)$ $\delta = 2(pq)^{1/2}[\arcsin \pi_x^{1/2} - \arcsin \pi_y^{1/2}]$	8.2

MASTER TABLE   5% Level, One-Tailed Test

POWER

Δ	99	95	90	80	70	60	50	40	30	20	10
0.01	157695	108215	85634	61823	47055	36031	27055	19363	12555	6453	1321
0.02	39417	27050	21405	15454	11763	9007	6764	4841	3139	1614	331
0.03	17514	12019	9511	6867	5227	4003	3006	2152	1396	718	148
0.04	9848	6758	5348	3861	2939	2251	1691	1210	785	404	84
0.05	6299	4323	3421	2470	1881	1440	1082	775	503	259	54
0.06	4372	3000	2375	1715	1305	1000	751	538	349	180	38
0.07	3209	2203	1744	1259	959	734	552	395	257	133	29
0.08	2455	1685	1334	963	734	562	422	303	197	102	23
0.09	1938	1330	1053	761	579	444	334	239	156	81	18
0.10	1568	1076	852	616	469	359	270	194	126	66	15
0.11	1294	889	704	508	387	297	223	160	104	54	13
0.12	1086	746	590	427	325	249	188	135	88	46	11
0.13	924	635	503	363	277	212	160	115	75	39	10
0.14	796	546	433	313	238	183	138	99	65	34	•
0.15	692	475	376	272	207	159	120	86	56	30	•
0.16	607	417	330	239	182	140	105	76	50	27	•
0.17	537	369	292	211	161	124	93	67	44	24	•
0.18	478	328	260	188	144	110	83	60	39	21	•
0.19	428	294	233	169	129	99	75	54	35	19	•
0.20	385	265	210	152	116	89	67	49	32	17	•

(continued)

MASTER TABLE 5% Level, One-Tailed Test Continued

POWER

Δ	99	95	90	80	70	60	50	40	30	20	10
0.22	317	218	173	125	96	74	56	40	27	15	·
0.24	265	182	144	105	80	62	47	34	23	12	·
0.26	224	154	122	89	68	52	40	29	19	11	·
0.28	192	132	105	76	58	45	34	25	17	10	·
0.30	166	114	91	66	51	39	30	22	15	·	·
0.32	145	100	79	58	44	34	26	19	13	·	·
0.34	127	88	70	51	39	30	23	17	12	·	·
0.36	113	78	62	45	35	27	20	15	10	·	·
0.38	100	69	55	40	31	24	18	14	·	·	·
0.40	89	62	49	36	28	21	16	12	·	·	·
0.45	69	48	38	28	21	17	13	10	·	·	·
0.50	54	37	30	22	17	13	10	·	·	·	·
0.55	43	30	24	17	14	11	·	·	·	·	·
0.60	34	24	19	14	11	·	·	·	·	·	·
0.65	28	19	16	12	·	·	·	·	·	·	·
0.70	23	16	13	10	·	·	·	·	·	·	·
0.75	18	13	10	·	·	·	·	·	·	·	·
0.80	15	10	·	·	·	·	·	·	·	·	·
0.85	12	·	·	·	·	·	·	·	·	·	·
0.90	·	·	·	·	·	·	·	·	·	·	·

1% Level, One-Tailed Test

Δ	POWER										
	99	95	90	80	70	60	50	40	30	20	10
0.01	216463	157695	130162	100355	81264	66545	54117	42972	32460	22044	10917
0.02	54106	39417	32535	25085	20313	16634	13528	10742	8117	5511	2730
0.03	24040	17514	14456	11146	9026	7391	6011	4773	3607	2449	1214
0.04	13517	9848	8128	6267	5075	4156	3380	2684	2029	1378	683
0.05	8646	6299	5200	4009	3247	2659	2163	1718	1298	882	437
0.06	6000	4372	3609	2783	2254	1846	1501	1192	901	612	304
0.07	4405	3209	2649	2043	1655	1355	1102	876	662	450	224
0.08	3369	2455	2027	1563	1266	1037	843	670	507	344	171
0.09	2660	1938	1600	1234	999	819	666	529	400	272	136
0.10	2152	1568	1295	998	809	663	539	428	324	220	110
0.11	1776	1294	1069	824	668	547	445	354	268	182	91
0.12	1490	1086	897	692	560	459	374	297	225	153	77
0.13	1268	924	763	589	477	391	318	253	191	130	65
0.14	1092	796	657	507	411	337	274	218	165	112	56
0.15	949	692	571	441	357	293	238	190	144	98	49
0.16	833	607	501	387	314	257	209	166	126	86	43
0.17	736	537	443	342	277	277	185	147	112	76	39
0.18	655	478	395	305	247	202	165	131	100	68	34
0.19	587	428	353	273	221	181	148	118	89	61	31
0.20	528	385	318	246	199	163	133	106	81	55	29

(continued)

107

1% Level, One-Tailed Test Continued

POWER

Δ	99	95	90	80	70	60	50	40	30	20	10
0.22	434	317	262	202	164	135	110	87	66	46	24
0.24	363	265	219	169	137	113	92	73	56	38	21
0.26	307	224	185	143	116	95	78	62	47	33	18
0.28	263	192	159	123	100	82	67	53	41	29	16
0.30	227	166	137	106	86	71	58	46	35	25	14
0.32	198	145	120	93	75	62	51	41	31	22	12
0.34	174	127	105	82	66	55	45	36	28	20	11
0.36	154	113	93	72	59	48	40	32	25	18	10
0.38	137	100	83	64	52	43	35	29	22	16	·
0.40	122	89	74	57	47	39	32	26	20	15	·
0.45	94	69	57	44	36	30	25	20	16	12	·
0.50	73	54	45	35	29	24	20	16	13	·	·
0.55	58	43	36	28	23	19	16	13	11	·	·
0.60	47	34	29	23	19	16	13	11	·	·	·
0.65	38	28	23	18	15	13	11	·	·	·	·
0.70	30	23	19	15	12	11	·	·	·	·	·
0.75	25	18	15	12	10	·	·	·	·	·	·
0.80	20	15	12	10	·	·	·	·	·	·	·
0.85	16	12	10	·	·	·	·	·	·	·	·
0.90	12	·	·	·	·	·	·	·	·	·	·

5% Level, Two-Tailed Test

Δ	99	95	90	80	70	60	50	40	30	20	10
					POWER						
0.01	183714	129940	105069	78485	61718	48986	38414	29125	20609	12508	4604
0.02	45920	32480	26263	19618	15428	12245	9603	7281	5152	3127	1152
0.03	20403	14431	11669	8717	6855	5441	4267	3236	2290	1390	513
0.04	11472	8115	6562	4902	3855	3060	2400	1820	1288	782	289
0.05	7338	5191	4197	3136	2466	1958	1536	1165	824	501	185
0.06	5093	3602	2913	2177	1712	1359	1066	809	573	348	129
0.07	3739	2645	2139	1598	1257	998	783	594	421	256	95
0.08	2860	2023	1636	1223	962	764	599	455	322	196	73
0.09	2257	1597	1292	965	759	603	473	359	255	155	58
0.10	1826	1292	1045	781	615	488	383	291	206	126	47
0.11	1508	1067	863	645	507	403	316	240	170	104	39
0.12	1265	895	724	541	426	338	266	202	143	88	33
0.13	1076	762	616	461	363	288	226	172	122	75	29
0.14	927	656	531	397	312	248	195	148	105	64	25
0.15	806	570	461	345	272	216	170	129	92	56	22
0.16	707	500	405	303	238	190	149	113	81	50	20
0.17	625	442	358	268	211	168	132	100	71	44	18
0.18	556	394	319	238	188	149	117	89	64	39	16
0.19	498	353	286	214	168	134	105	80	57	35	15
0.20	449	318	257	192	152	121	95	72	52	32	13

(continued)

5% Level, Two-Tailed Test Continued

POWER

Δ	99	95	90	80	70	60	50	40	30	20	10
0.22	369	261	212	158	125	99	78	60	43	27	11
0.24	308	218	177	133	105	83	66	50	36	23	10
0.26	261	185	150	112	89	71	56	43	31	20	·
0.28	223	159	128	96	76	61	48	37	27	17	·
0.30	193	137	111	83	66	53	42	32	23	15	·
0.32	169	120	97	73	58	46	36	28	21	13	·
0.34	148	105	85	64	51	41	32	25	18	12	·
0.36	131	93	75	57	45	36	29	22	16	11	·
0.38	116	83	67	51	40	32	26	20	15	10	·
0.40	104	74	60	45	36	29	23	18	13	·	·
0.45	80	57	46	35	28	22	18	14	11	·	·
0.50	62	45	36	27	22	18	14	11	·	·	·
0.55	50	35	29	22	18	14	12	·	·	·	·
0.60	40	29	23	18	14	12	10	·	·	·	·
0.65	32	23	19	15	12	10	·	·	·	·	·
0.70	26	19	15	12	10	·	·	·	·	·	·
0.75	21	15	13	10	·	·	·	·	·	·	·
0.80	17	12	10	·	·	·	·	·	·	·	·
0.85	13	10	·	·	·	·	·	·	·	·	·
0.90	10	·	·	·	·	·	·	·	·	·	·

1% Level, Two-Tailed Test

	POWER										
Δ	99	95	90	80	70	60	50	40	30	20	10
0.01	240299	178131	148785	116783	96109	80039	66346	53937	42082	30074	16752
0.02	60064	44525	37190	29191	24024	20007	16584	13483	10520	7518	4188
0.03	26687	19783	16524	12970	10674	8890	7369	5991	4675	3341	1862
0.04	15005	11123	9291	7293	6002	4999	4144	3369	2629	1879	1047
0.05	9598	7115	5943	4665	3840	3198	2651	2155	1682	1202	670
0.06	6661	4938	4125	3238	2665	2220	1840	1496	1168	835	466
0.07	4890	3625	3028	2377	1957	1630	1351	1099	858	613	342
0.08	3740	2773	2316	1819	1497	1247	1034	841	656	469	262
0.09	2952	2189	1829	1436	1182	984	816	664	518	371	207
0.10	2389	1771	1480	1162	956	797	661	537	420	300	168
0.11	1972	1462	1221	959	789	658	545	444	346	248	139
0.12	1654	1227	1025	805	663	552	458	372	291	208	117
0.13	1407	1044	872	685	564	470	390	317	248	177	100
0.14	1212	898	751	590	485	405	336	273	213	153	86
0.15	1054	781	653	513	422	352	292	238	186	133	75
0.16	924	685	573	450	371	309	256	209	163	117	66
0.17	817	606	506	398	328	273	227	185	144	104	58
0.18	727	539	451	354	292	243	202	164	129	92	52
0.19	651	483	404	317	261	218	181	147	115	83	47
0.20	586	435	364	286	235	196	163	133	104	75	42

(continued)

111

1% Level, Two-Tailed Test Continued

POWER

Δ	99	95	90	80	70	60	50	40	30	20	10
0.22	482	358	299	235	194	162	134	109	86	62	35
0.24	403	299	250	196	162	135	112	92	72	52	30
0.26	341	253	212	166	137	115	95	78	61	44	26
0.28	292	217	181	143	118	98	82	67	52	38	23
0.30	252	187	157	123	102	85	71	58	45	33	20
0.32	220	163	137	108	89	74	62	51	40	30	18
0.34	193	144	120	95	78	65	54	45	35	26	15
0.36	171	127	106	84	69	58	48	39	31	24	15
0.38	152	113	94	74	62	52	43	35	29	21	13
0.40	135	101	84	67	55	46	38	32	26	19	12
0.45	104	77	65	51	42	36	30	25	20	15	10
0.50	81	61	51	40	33	28	24	20	16	12	.
0.55	64	48	40	32	27	23	19	16	13	10	.
0.60	52	39	32	26	22	19	16	15	11	.	.
0.65	41	31	27	21	18	15	13	11	.	.	.
0.70	33	25	22	17	15	13	11	.	.	.	.
0.75	27	21	17	14	12	10	.	.	.	.	.
0.80	22	17	14	11	.	.	.	.	.	.	.
0.85	17	13	11	.	.	.	.	.	.	.	.
0.90	13	10	.	.	.	.	.	.	.	.	.

References

Bartko, J. J. (1976). "On various intraclass correlation reliability coefficients," *Psychological Bulletin 83*, 762-765.

Binstock, M., Krakow, D., Stamler, J., Reiff, J., Persky, V., Liu, K., and Moss, D. (1983). "Coffee and pancreatic cancer: An analysis of international mortality data," *American Journal of Epidemiology 118(5)*, 630-640.

Boomsma, A. (1977). "Comparing approximations of confidence intervals for the product-moment correlation coefficient," *Statistica Neerlandica 31*, 179-185.

Brodman, K., Erdmann, A. J., and Wolff, H. G. (1949). *Cornell Medical Index—Health Questionnaire Manual*, New York: Cornell University Medical College.

Chaubey, Y. P., and Mudholkar, G. S. (1978). "A new approximation for Fisher's Z," *Australian Journal of Statistics 20*, 250-256.

Cochran, W. G. (1940). "Note on an approximate formula for the significance level of Z," *Annals of Mathematical Statistics 11*, 93-95.

Cohen, J. (1977). *Statistical Power Analysis for the Behavioral Sciences* (Rev. ed.). New York: Academic Press.

Cohen, J. (1983). "The cost of dichotomization," *Applied Psychological Measurement 7*, 249-253.

Fieller, F. E., Hartley, H. O., and Pearson, E. S. (1957). "Tests for rank correlation coefficients. I," *Biometrika 44*, 470-481.

Fieller, E. C., and Pearson, E. S. (1961). "Tests for rank correlation coefficients. II," *Biometrika 48*, 29-40.

Fisher, R. A. (1921). "On the 'probable error' of a coefficient of correlation deduced from a small sample," *Metron 1*, Part 4, 32.

Goldstein, A. (1964). *Biostatistics: An Introductory Text*, New York: MacMillan.

Gordon, C., Emerson, A. R., and Simpson, J. (1959). "The Cornell Medical Index Questionnaire as a measure of health in socio-medical research," *Journal of Gerontology 14*, 305-308.

Haggard, E. A. (1958). *Intraclass Correlation and the Analysis of Variance*, New York: Dryden Press.

Hedges, L.V., and Olkin, I. (1985). *Statistical Methods in Meta Analysis*, New York: Academic Press.

Kraemer, H. C. (1973). "Improved approximation to the non-null distribution of the correlation coefficient," *Journal of the American Statistical Association 68*, 1004-1008.

Kraemer, H. C. (1975). "On estimation and hypothesis testing problems for correlation coefficients," *Psychometrika 40*, 473-485.

Kraemer, H. C. (1980). "Robustness of the distribution theory of the product-moment correlation coefficient," *Journal of Educational Statistics 5(2)*, 115-128.

Kraemer, H. C. (1981). "Extension of Feldt's approach to testing homogeneity of coefficients of reliability," *Psychometrika 46(1)*, 41-45.

Kraemer, H. C. (1985). "A strategy to teach the concept and application of power of statistical tests in an elementary course," *Journal of Educational Statistics, 10(3)*, 173-195.

Kraemer, H. C., and Paik, M. (1979). "A central t approximation to the non-central t distribution," *Technometrics 21*, 357-360.

LaVecchia, C., Franceschi, S., Decarli, A., Gentile, A., Liati, P., Regallo, M., Tognoni, G. (1984). "Coffee drinking and the risk of epithelial ovarian cancer," *International Journal of Cancer 33(5)*, 559-562.

Marrett, L. D., Walter, S. D., and Meigs, J. W. (1983). "Coffee drinking and bladder cancer in Connecticut," *American Journal of Epidemiology 117(2)*, 113-127.

Morgan, W. A. (1939). "A test for the significance of the difference between two variances in a sample from a normal bivariate population," *Biometrika 31*, 13-19.

Pearson, E. S., and Hartley, H. O. (1962). *Biometrika Tables for Statisticians*, Vol. 1, Cambridge: University Press.

Phillips, R. L., and Snowdon, D. A. (1983). "Association of meat and coffee use with cancers of the large bowel, breast, and prostate among Seventh-Day Adventists," *Cancer Research 43(5 Suppl)*, 2403-2408.

Pitman, E. J. G. (1939). "A note on normal correlation," *Biometrika 31*, 9-12.

Scheffe, H. (1959). *The Analysis of Variance*, New York: Wiley, chap. 10.

Siegel, S. (1956). *Non-Parametric Statistics for the Behavioral Sciences*, New York: McGraw-Hill.

Snowdon, D. A., and Phillips, R. L. (1984). "Coffee consumption and risk of fatal cancers," *American Journal of Public Health 74(8)*, 820-823.

Whitsett, T. L., Manion, C. V., Christensen, H. D. (1984). "Cardiovascular effects of coffee and caffeine," *American Journal of Cardiology 53(7)*, 918-922.

Williams, P. T., Wood, P. D., Vianizan, K. M., Albers, J. J., Garay, S. C., and Taylor, C. B. (1985). "Coffee intake and elevated cholesterol and apolipoprotein B levels in men," *Journal of the American Medical Association 253(10)*, 1407-1411.

Index

About the Authors

Helena Chmura Kraemer, Professor of Biostatistics in the Department of Psychiatry and Behavioral Sciences at Stanford University and by courtesy in the Division of Biostatistics, earned her B.A. in mathematics from Smith College, attended Manchester University on a Fulbright scholarship, and received her Ph.D. in statistics from Stanford University. Her specific research interests include investigating testing and estimation techniques for correlation, most recently 2×2 association; developing valid and reliable methods for behavioral observation; constructing new mathematical models for specific problems in behavioral and clinical research, such as measuring memory loss or estimating gestational age; and developing guidelines for efficient research design using human subjects. She has published extensively in the behavioral as well as statistical literature, with articles appearing in *Psychological Bulletin, Developmental Psychology, American Anthropologist, Child Development, Behavioral Science, Contemporary Psychology,* and *Archives of General Psychiatry,* as well as in *Psychometrika, Journal of Mathematical Psychology, Journal of the American Statistical Association, Biometrics, Biometrika,* and *Technometrics.*

Sue Thiemann is a biostatistician in the Department of Psychiatry and Behavioral Sciences at Stanford University. She received her B.A. in linguistics and philosophy from Harvard University and her M.S. in statistics from Stanford University. She has worked primarily in psychiatric clinical research and has published articles in this field in various journals, including *Psychiatry Research, Biological Psychiatry, Neurobiology of Aging, Archives of General Psychiatry,* and *Current Therapeutic Research.*

120